THE LAST BLUES PREACHER

THE LAST BLUES PREACHER

Reverend Clay Evans, Black Lives, and the Faith that Woke the Nation

Zach Mills

Fortress Press

Minneapolis

THE LAST BLUES PREACHER
Reverend Clay Evans, Black Lives, and the Faith that Woke the
Nation

Cover design: Alisha Lofgren

Print ISBN: 978-1-5064-2817-8
eBook ISBN: 978-1-5064-4655-4

The paper used in this publication meets the minimum
requirements of American National Standard for Information
Sciences — Permanence of Paper for Printed Library Materials,
ANSI Z329.48-1984.

Manufactured in the U.S.A.

Contents

PREFACE

The first time I met Rev. Clay Evans was on a brisk summer afternoon in Chicago on Thursday, August 25, 2011. The air outside that morning was cool, as if fall had stolen a few weeks of summer. We sat outside on a patio deck. We had finished all appropriate introductions. I was attempting to communicate my reluctance to take on the responsibility of writing Reverend Evans's biography. At the time, I was serving as an associate minister of a church in Chicago's Hyde Park neighborhood and had many weekly responsibilities. I worried that my busy schedule as a minister would not leave much free time to write a biography. In addition to my ministerial duties, I was in the final stages of writing a thesis for a master of arts program in Vanderbilt University's Graduate Department of Religion. I still had a significant amount of writing to do before my thesis was complete. But more than anxiety about my busy schedule, I felt—if I'm being honest—inadequate for the task. I was unsure of myself. Surely there were more experienced writers who could tell Reverend Evans's story. After all, I hadn't even thought about writing a biography. I looked at Reverend Evans and gave my best speech. I confessed my inexperience. I highlighted my weaknesses. I voiced my concerns.

Reverend Evans looked at me and said calmly, "I want you to be concerned but not worried. You can't disappoint me. Full speed ahead." That was his mantra that morning: "Full speed ahead." Despite my reservations, my gut was telling me that I should say yes. And full speed ahead we all went.

A few weeks later, we agreed to meet at the home of Reverend Evans's daughter Gail. There I would conduct my first official interview with Reverend Evans. I pulled up to the handsome light-blue house on 116th Place on Chicago's South Side. Rain drizzled outside. Only a few slivers of sunlight managed to escape the overcast sky. I shut my car door behind me. Raindrops pattered gently on the canopy of tree leaves above me, where they slowed in speed and diminished in substance before dripping on my head. I looked at the house. I knew a special moment in my life would blossom as soon as I stepped through the front door. I was a little nervous, because I was a few minutes late. The rain and a slow-moving train blocking a nearby intersection had delayed my arrival. Still, Reverend Evans's daughter greeted me warmly at the door. I apologized for being late. She gave me a hug and whispered graciously to me that everyone else had walked in just moments before I had. She, too, had been delayed by the weather on the way from work to meet us at her home. I felt relieved knowing we all ended up arriving almost evenly tardy.

I walked into the dining room. Reverend Evans was sitting at the head of the table nearest to where I entered the room. There were five of us. I could sense we were about to embark upon a very important journey. I felt the weight of the task before us. Not that I hadn't before. But just being there, sitting at that table, looking at that dedicated group of people, made me realize that we were there because of a life that had inspired so many more people than were present in that room. I could feel the weight of that moment as I looked upon the faces of those seated at that dining-room table. At the time, we were all still mostly strangers to one another. Yet we gathered eagerly in spite of busy work schedules and many other obligations. The energy in that room was palpable. The task before us was daunting. And my task as the chief writer—to tell the story of a man whose ministry had helped define the culture of an entire city and the gospel music industry—seemingly impossible. It was a heavy burden that I alone would have to endure.

Suddenly, unexpectedly, that weight lifted from me. I didn't feel as alone. I opened my laptop. I placed a tape recorder in front of Reverend Evans. I took a deep breath. And I pressed record. "Thank you so much, Reverend Evans, for your time," I said. "I want to ask you some questions about your life and your ministry at Fellowship Missionary Baptist Church." Reverend Evans grinned gently, almost as if he could sense the mixture of excitement and anxiety coursing through me. "Go ahead, Reverend," he said in that low, gravely, resolute voice. "Full speed ahead."

AUTHOR'S NOTE

What helps make *The Last Blues Preacher* so special is the host of quotes friends, family, church members, and colleagues contributed in the telling of Rev. Clay Evans's story. I want to thank each person whose quote appears in this project for investing the time to be interviewed. Each person's contribution added vibrant testimony about Rev. Clay Evans and the significance of his ministry. I would like to also thank Patty Nolan Fitzgerald and Mary Prendergast for the interviews they conducted when my work schedule and other obligations did not allow me to facilitate interviews. Both Patty and Mary invested an enormous amount of time coordinating logistics for interviews, conducting research, and offering insightful perspectives during my interviews with Rev. Clay Evans.

Quotes from the following people were obtained from interviews that took place in person, over the phone, or through written correspondence:

Timuel Black: Black is a long-time South Side activist, educator, and Chicago historian.

Chuck Bowen: Bowen served as a former aid to Chicago Mayor Richard M. Daley.

Dr. Alexander Doolas: Doolas is a retired Chicago physician who successfully performed Rev. Clay Evans's pancreatic cancer surgery in 2001.

Michael Evans: Michael is a son of Rev. Clay Evans.

Pharis Evans: Pharis is a brother of Rev. Clay Evans.

Faith Evans: Faith is a daughter of Rev. Clay Evans.

The Honorable Minister Louis Farrakhan: Farrakhan is the leader of the Nation of Islam.

Rev. Henry O. Hardy: Hardy is pastor emeritus of Cosmopolitan Community Church in Chicago.

Dr. Johari Jabir: Jabir is Associate Professor of African American Studies at the University of Illinois at Chicago.

The Reverend Jesse L. Jackson: Jackson is the founder of Rainbow/PUSH, a long-time civil rights leader, and a close friend of Rev. Clay Evans.

Reverend Charles Jenkins: Jenkins is the senior pastor of Fellowship Missionary Baptist Church and Evans's successor.

Jack Malone: Malone is long-time chaplain serving Cook County Jail in Chicago.

Rev. Dr. Harolynn McIntosh: McIntosh served for seven years as one of the pastors in the children's ministry at Fellowship Missionary Baptist Church.

Reverend Otis Moss Jr.: Moss is a long-time civil rights activist who offered key leadership within the Southern Christian Leadership Conference during the 1960s.

Loretta Oliver: Oliver was a long-time soloist in Fellowship Missionary Baptist Church's two-hundred-voice choir.

Father Michael Pfleger: Pfleger is the senior pastor of The Faith Community of Saint Sabina in Chicago.

Dr. Harold Pye: Pye, who passed away in 2016, was married to Rev. Clay Evans's daughter Gail C. Evans and was the owner of a medical facility, HTP Associates.

Gail C. Evans-Pye: Gail is a daughter of Rev. Clay Evans.

Governor Pat Quinn: Quinn is a former governor of Illinois who was in office when he was interviewed for this project.

Lou Della Evans Reid: Lou Della is a sister of Rev. Clay Evans and served as choir director at Fellowship Missionary Baptist Church from 1950 to 2000.

Congressman Bobby Rush: Rush is an Illinois Democratic congressman.

Michael Shaw: Shaw was a long-time pianist at Fellowship Missionary Baptist Church.

Mary Stinson: Stinson was a long-time soloist in the two-hundred-voice choir at Fellowship Missionary Baptist Church.

The Reverend Dr. Stephen J. Thurston: Thurston is the senior pastor of New Covenant Missionary Baptist Church in Chicago.

Eddie Vrdolyak: Vrdolyak is a former Chicago alderman.

Mickey "Royal" Warren: Warren was a long-time organist at Fellowship Missionary Baptist Church.

Rev. Dr. Don Sharp: Sharp is pastor of Faith Tabernacle Baptist Church in Chicago.

ACKNOWLEDGMENTS

To my parents, Janet and Hank, I am forever grateful for the unwavering enthusiasm you provided during the eight years I spent writing *The Last Blues Preacher*. Your constant support, counsel, and encouraging words comforted me during the difficult days of this project. And your excitement about this project made the best days of this project even better! To my siblings Jennifer, Josh, Molly, and Daniel, thank you for listening to me over the years as I worked through the details of this project. To my attorney Alexis (Lexy) Payne, without your counsel and unwavering advocacy this project would not have been possible. To Antonio Casey, thank you for all the wisdom and enthusiasm you've shared to help this project. To Lisa Kloskin, Katie Clifford, Layne Johnson, and the entire Fortress Press staff, I am grateful for all the time, talent, and labor each of you invested to make this project so strong. To Dr. Victor Anderson, who served as the first editor of this project, thank you for your editorial genius that rescued this project from becoming electronic compost in my computer's trash! To Rev. Clay Evans, I am so thankful for your wisdom, humor, and for the exciting adventure that *The Last Blues Preacher* became. Finally, I am grateful to God for giving me the mysterious energy, enthusiasm, and persistence that pushed me, late at night and early in the morning, and in the face of every single obstacle I encountered, to press on until this project was completed!

INTRODUCTION

When Rev. Clay Evans journeyed to Chicago from Brownsville, Tennessee, in 1945, he brought the rich cultural and religious traditions of black southern culture. One of these traditions, a folk orality, had dramatically shaped Evans's voice. This orality—a vast matrix of speaking tones, singing techniques, styles of communication, vernacular expressions, and rhetorical devices—shaped the ways black southern migrants in Chicago expressed themselves in secular and religious spaces. The Reverend Otis Moss Jr. recalled the uniqueness of Evans's voice: "He was gifted in music and song," Moss said. "He had the ability to touch and attract people from all levels of experience. And he had the ability to take his gifts in music and song and incorporate that with the gospel of Jesus Christ and the building of a great and dynamic church. His church became known as literally a spiritual powerhouse for great leadership, dynamic preaching, and great music."[1]

Evans organized Fellowship Missionary Baptist Church on Sunday, September 10, 1950. During Evans's fifty years as senior pastor of "The Ship," as it was famously known in Chicago and throughout the United States, Fellowship Church became a center of healing that offered a soothing balm for the many blues plaguing its members. Each Sunday and throughout the week, Fellowship became a place where attendees' ultimate concerns—their joys and sorrows—were articulated artfully with the raw acuity of the blues singer and the audacious, sophisticated hope of the gospel preacher.

Music, in particular, was a primary avenue through which healing was administered at the "The Ship." Minister Louis Farrakhan reflected on the unique cultural contribution southern migrants like Evans made to the religious worship experience in Chicago in the mid-1900s. These individuals, Farrakhan said, brought a creative mixture of sacred and secular musical sensibilities along with a fiery passion for congregational worship:

> Well, I'll put it like this, we as a people coming through the hardship of the transatlantic slave trade and the evil of slavery, what did we have on the plantation to comfort us, but our music, our songs. So out of the depth of our pain came "swing low sweet chariot." "Deep river my soul is over Jordan. I want to cross over into campground." Those spirituals comforted us. So we've always been a people of song. Always been a people of dance. And no matter where we are we've always been a people of praise. So my brother's unique voice coming up out of the South . . . it's the people of Mississippi, Alabama, Tennessee, Arkansas, Georgia, Louisiana fleeing the pain of the farm as a sharecropper, fleeing

that to come North to find refuge in this new city, Chicago. Rev. Evans was one of those who came from the South to the North and what did he bring with him? He brought with him the songs of praise and the uniqueness of his voice. It had a stamp that when you heard it, "That's Rev. Evans." The uniqueness of his style of delivery, it was pure Clay Evans.[2]

By the time black southern migrants like Evans arrived in Chicago in the middle of the twentieth century, both the blues and gospel music had emerged as primary vehicles for analyzing and expressing African Americans' experiences of suffering and resilience in urban settings. As scholar Wallace D. Best argues: "The content of the blues has served as a lyrical map of the African American urban world. . . . The gospel music of Chicago . . . revealed a similar lyrical map with a similar take on the African American experience in Chicago."[3]

Preachers like Clay Evans were the working-class orators of the black experience who intuitively merged the blues and gospel to express the hurts and hopes of their people.[4] This form of preaching has been described and understood culturally as "blues preaching." Blues preaching was a spirituals-and-blues-inspired tradition of preaching that circulated throughout various parts of the South in the late nineteenth and twentieth centuries. Blues preachers became significant pillars in African American communities in northern cities like Chicago and Detroit as their ministries both uplifted and informed the congregations they served. The skills of the blues preacher were not acquired in a classroom or the result of some innate vocal genius. The blues preacher's skills were forged in the fiery furnace of the racism, brutality, and suffering African Americans experienced in the South in the early 1900s.

Between 1900 and 1930, whites lynched a black person at least twice a year in the seventeen counties making up the Mississippi Delta, not far from Evans's hometown of Brownsville, Tennessee.[5] African Americans' constant fear of the violent retaliation they would experience if they publically opposed racism forced many in the South to internalize their fears and rage in silence. This psychological and physical terror nevertheless sponsored an economy of hope and resilience voiced in the black expressive culture of the blues. As the father of black theology of liberation, James H. Cone, argues: "The blues recognize that black people have been hurt and scared by the brutalities of white society. But there is hope in what Richard Wright calls the 'endemic capacity to live.' This hope provided the strength to survive, and the openness to the intensity of life's pains without being destroyed by them."[6] In other words, through the blues, people whose bodies had been strained and drained from slavery and its aftermath resolved to resiliently belt out their private, formerly inaudible sighs. Houston Baker Jr. shares Cone's sentiments. Baker argues the blues, or rather, the many material elements making up and giving voice to the blues—a growling guitar, a raspy voice lamenting lost love, or the bitter lyrics bemoaning life as a sharecropper, for example—are all musical personifications of concrete life experience. In short, the blues summarize the vast dimensions of African Americans' experiences, especially experiences of grief, suffering, and loss.

Through their sermons, blues preachers used the powerful expressions about life found in black musical traditions like the blues and gospel to educate, encourage, and inspire African Americans. Blues preachers like Evans were symbols of possibility among black communities during a time the United States had initiated local and national policies to oppress African Americans. In the face of such systematic efforts to inhibit black progress, Rev. Clay Evans dared in his preaching to mobilize African Americans in collective quests toward more abundant life. In fact, communal movement beyond oppressive boundaries served as Fellowship's primary identity and mission. Evans's constant circulation of the metaphors of "fellowship" and "ship" in his preaching and singing opposed national policies of discrimination and asserted more positive representations of black identity and citizenship. The theme of "fellowship" was evoked regularly during Fellowship's worship services. This theme conveyed two primary characteristics of Fellowship's worship experience represented in the church's name: radical communion and radical mobility. Evans's use of the theme of "fellowship" throughout his fifty-year ministry served as an invitation for people to seek out communion and mobility. A brief discussion about these two characteristics of "fellowship" will be helpful here.

The communal aspect of Fellowship's mission was conveyed regularly during the church's worship services and, consequently, during the church's weekly radio broadcast, *What a Fellowship Hour.*[7] The radio broadcast opened with Fellowship's choir singing the theme song, "Leaning on the Everlasting Arms." This cherished Protestant hymn testifies about the rewards of seeking more genuine communion with God. The song's first verse includes a phrase that Evans would use to rhetorically construct Fellowship's mission in terms of unity:

What a fellowship, what a joy divine,
Leaning on the everlasting arms;
What a blessedness, what a peace is mine,
Leaning on the everlasting arms.[8]

The lyrics and logic of this song became lenses through which Evans interpreted and articulated Fellowship's identity and mission. For Evans, the rewards of fellowship with God conveyed in "Leaning on the Everlasting Arms" had implications for interpersonal relationships, or fellowship, between human beings. Evans's signature catchphrase during the beginning of worship services at "The Ship" fused both divine and human implications of fellowship:

What a ship! What a ship! What a ship! It's a kin-ship. It's friend-ship. It's a relation-ship, and all that means is, what a fellowship! Are you on board?! I say are you on board?![9]

For Evans, Fellowship was a church in which people could

forge closer relationships with one another as they sought closer relationships with God. Evans's particular use of "ship" imagery served as a metaphorical link to the images of ships portrayed as places of refuge throughout the Holy Bible. Both Old and New Testament Scriptures contain dramatic depictions of ships as vessels of protection. In Genesis, Noah's ark protected human and animal passengers from a catastrophic flood. Similarly, in Mark 4:35–41, Jesus, a passenger with his disciples on a small ship, prevents a sudden storm from capsizing the vessel. In both of these Scriptures, the ship serves as a symbol of communal salvation—a place where various communities find protection and hope for new life. Thus, communion, the cultivation of positive relationships with others regardless of race or religion, became a central aspect of Fellowship's identity and mission.

Evans believed strongly that since communion with God provided the basic resources necessary for the flourishing of life, then fellowship between people should also provide similar benefits. In other words, Evans's emphasis on the theme of "communion" provided for members a model for how to lovingly relate to one another. African American studies professor Johari Jabir offers a compelling analysis of Fellowship's theme song, "Leaning on the Everlasting Arms," also known as "What a Fellowship." Jabir said, "Listening to the church's hard swinging version of the Protestant staple, 'What A Fellowship' reminds me of Paul Gilroy's discussion of the ship imagery in the Black Atlantic memory of music." For Jabir, Evans's use of "ship" imagery conveyed a mission of gathering a disenfranchised, oppressed black diaspora for the purpose of healing and mobilization. Jabir explains further:

> Just as enslaved Africans imagined an alternate "ship" of Zion as a signification on slave ships, Rev. Evans took hold of the memory of that ship of violence, terror, and irreparable rupture, and he turned it into a vessel of freedom, love, and acceptance. A giant in the forest of black preachers, Rev. Evans' labor as a caring pastor connected to the needs of people is important to note. What I find so remarkable about Rev. Evans is the way in which he allowed the blues to serve as the organic root for his preaching, pastorate, and activism. Stylistically, his preaching is steeped in the bluesman preachers of the late nineteenth and early twentieth centuries. He preached a theology of the blues that affirmed the suffering, liberation, and nobility of black people as divinely human in a society that tried to denigrate their existence. As a priest charged to care for the community and as a soldier of love on the battlefield for freedom Rev. Evans created a "whosoever church" founded upon relationality. This church was a house of blues where anybody and everybody could enter in and find healing and refuge.[10]

While the mission of "The Ship" celebrates communion, it also emphasizes *mobility*. Ships sail. They travel. They embark. They venture to new worlds. And they bring passengers with them. Despite racist national policies designed to contain African Americans during the Cold War era, Evans's circulation of "ship" imagery encouraged radical figurative and literal movement among Fellowship's passengers. Whether listening by radio or worshiping in person, once on board "The Ship," Fellowship's passengers became a people on the move, a people together on their way to someplace better. Evans's frequent call to those in person or listening over the radio to get on board "The Ship" was an invitation to participate in the experience of a communal odyssey that Fellowship, a church journeying to a new land, promised to offer each passenger. Those who were brave enough to get on board soon found themselves on a journey, a beautiful journey, toward healing and hope and the best of themselves. Even after all these years, they can still hear their captain calling, "All aboard!"

NOTES

1. Rev. Otis Moss Jr., interview by Patty Nolan-Fitzgerald, 2012, Trinity United Church of Christ, Chicago.

2. Minister Louis Farrakhan, interview by Zach Mills, 2012, Rev. Clay Evans's home, Chicago.

3. Wallace D. Best, *Passionately Human, No Less Divine: Religion and Culture in Black Chicago, 1915–1952* (Princeton: Princeton University Press, 2005), 110.

4. Best, *Passionately Human*, 110.

5. Nick Salvatore, *Singing in a Strange Land: C. L. Franklin, the Black Church, and the Transformation of America* (Urbana: University of Illinois Press, 2006), 5.

6. James H. Cone, *The Spirituals and the Blues: An Interpretation* (New York: Seabury, 1972), 140.

7. Evans's weekly *What a Fellowship Hour* radio broadcast first aired in 1952 and continued uninterrupted until Evans's retired in 2000.

8. Delores Carpenter and Nolan E. Williams Jr., eds., *The African American Heritage Hymnal* (Chicago: Gia, 2001), 371.

9. This quote can be heard in two virtually identical iterations in several YouTube videos of Fellowship's worship services. One video ("Rev. Clay EVANS What a Fellowship Hour OPENING," video, 4:29, uploaded by BrothaRollins, August 5, 2007, http://tinyurl.com/yd9a4ja6) is from an earlier worship service. Another video ("What a Fellowship [Celebration Version]," video, 3:04, uploaded by fstanley35, April 10, 2008, http://tinyurl.com/y8dkm2nf) was recorded in September 2005, after Evans retired from Fellowship but presided over Fellowship's reunion concert, which brought back choir members that had sung with the church's choir when Evans served as pastor.

10. Henry Louis Gates Jr.'s *The Signifying Monkey* (Oxford: Oxford University Press, 1988) offers a helpful description of vernacular signification in Afro-American cultures as a rhetorical practice.

PART I

BEGINNINGS

WHO ME?

Rev. Clay Evans will never read a word of this story. Not one word. He would; he just can't. His eyesight isn't what it used to be. It's a hard truth, a difficult reality. But Reverend Evans won't ever read his story on these published pages. No matter. He knows the story pretty well. After all, it's his story. Actually, Reverend Evans's life has been more like an exciting adventure, filled with tragedies and joys, friends and enemies, villains and heroes, victories and defeats. And now this adventure is retold for you, in hopes that it will impart some important lessons. Lessons, Reverend Evans would say, to inspire you to be the best version of yourself. Lessons to challenge you to extend greater measures of openness, generosity, and mercy to those you encounter—yes even, and especially, your enemies! Lessons, he'd say, to inspire you to show greater humility—yes, definitely to those with whom you disagree! Lessons to reconcile you with others and yourself. That's always been Reverend Evans's hope for this project. "If this book doesn't help encourage someone else, if it doesn't inspire them, give them hope, or draw them closer to God," he'd often say to me, "then there's no point writing it." So here is Rev. Clay Evans's great adventure in life and ministry, shared now with you for the sake of the better world you can create if you're open enough, loving enough, courageous enough, and humble enough to learn the lessons within these pages.

During his fifty years as a senior pastor, Rev. Clay Evans comforted thousands of souls. However, the only way to tell Evans's story properly is to begin with the very first soul his ministry ever touched. It's earlier than one might think, earlier than even he remembers. The first time Clay Evans eased the agony of a burdened soul went something like this:

DECEMBER 1927—It was December 23, 1927. In Haywood County on a rural farm in Brownsville, Tennessee, a shy two-and-a-half-year-old boy named Clay scurried across the shabby floor of a sharecropping family's small kitchen. His mother, Estanauly, looked lovingly on. She pondered, "What a strange child!" She knew it. Her husband Henry and the rest of the family knew it. Even all the neighbors knew it. Clay's third birthday was just sixth months away, and he hadn't spoken a single word. Not one. Instead, he communicated nonverbally—through body language, facial expressions, and smiles and frowns. Or he used an assortment of noises, like groaning or grunting. But he never spoke words. He couldn't. Clay Evans was a sickly child. Everyone knew it. "My mother was very burdened about that," he recalled. "She prayed and prayed and prayed that

I would talk." To ease the weight of such a terrible burden, his mother often looked heavenward for strength. Writing about the intensity of Estanauly's struggle raising a son with health problems, author Dorothy June Rose declared, "Clay had been the supreme test of her faith. A sickly baby, he taxed her energy and often kept her in anxious vigil through long and sleepless nights."[1] There were moments when Estanauly and Henry Evans faced the painful possibility that their son might never speak.

One autumn day several months earlier, Estanauly had sat on the porch steps of the Evanses' home in Brownsville with her two friends, Ellie and Pearl. Estanauly, then a thirty-one-year-old mother of four who was sixth months pregnant with her fifth child, watched Ellie and Pearl's children play a game of hide-and-go-seek while little Clay sat silently. Ellie and Pearl looked at Clay. Then they looked at Estanauly with concerned eyes. Finally, Pearl gathered the courage to break the silence:

> "Whatcha goin to do 'bout that baby of yours there, Estanauly?" Pearl asked. "Over two years old now and just sits there quiet as a little field mouse."
>
> Ellie also chimed in. "Do you suppose he's ever goin' to talk, Estanauly?" she asked.[2]

Estanauly gazed fondly at Clay. Refusing to hide her uncertainty, she replied simply, *"I don't know."* Doubt filled her eyes, but only for a moment. Still gazing at her happy baby boy, Estanauly beamed brightly. It was the hopeful smile of a woman of faith who believed God could, somehow, do the impossible. Encouraged by this hope, she turned back to her friends, more certain this time, and responded:

> "All I know, he's in the good Lord's hands. He was a hard time borning and sick more than well his whole first year. Henry 'n I was sure we'd lose him many a night. But the good Lord brought him through, and brought him through for a purpose. If the Lord give us a dumb baby, well He give him to us for a reason. And if the Lord wants Clay to talk, well, He'll just have to make that happen, too. Ain't nothin goes on He's not in charge of. And that's just good enough for me."[3]

In the meantime, family members adjusted. They learned to decipher Clay's many nonverbal cues. Estanauly continued to pray for her mute son's deliverance. So many nights she prayed. And so many mornings little Clay woke up still quiet as a field mouse. But then, two days before Christmas in 1927, her prayers were answered. Estanauly was sitting with friends at the Evanses' kitchen table, watching Clay scurry silently about. Though the Evans family had very little money, Estanauly was determined to give her children at least one homemade gift for Christmas. She had ripped the seams out of her blue skirt, the prettiest garment she owned, and made a dress for her daughter, Gladys. Estanauly's friends scolded her for ruining her skirt. But Estanauly beamed with pride. "And besides," she said, justifying her sacrifice to her friends, "there was enough left over to make this little stuffed dog for Clay." Right then, little Clay looked up at his mother, wide-eyed with anticipation, and interjected, *"Who? Me?"* The words came so clearly, so unexpectedly. Estanauly's heart raced. God had answered her prayers!

When Evans retold the story of the time he had overcome his struggle to speak, he evoked the biblical character Moses. Moses, Evans testified, also had struggled with speech. The third and fourth chapters of the Old Testament book of Exodus narrate God calling Moses to free the Israelites from the oppressive rule of a pharaoh who was holding them as slaves in Egypt. Because of anxieties about his own limitations as a leader, Moses responded to God by saying, "Who am I that I should go to Pharaoh, and bring the Israelites out of Egypt?" (Exodus 3:11, NRSV). Evans has always interpreted Moses's struggle in Exodus through the lens of his own struggle with speech. There, in Moses's story, Evans found an encouraging similarity. "Moses also said, 'Who? Me?'" Evans concluded proudly.

Evans credited his mother's regular prayer life with his emancipation from muteness: "She really prayed that her son would be able to talk . . . my mother was a real saint." When she heard her son finally speak words, Estanauly dropped to her knees. She wrapped Clay in her arms. Tears streamed down both cheeks. "Thank you, Lord," she whispered. "Thank you for letting this child of mine talk. Now please, I pray, give me the wisdom to guide him so his voice is ever raised in your service."[4]

Born on June 23, 1925, just over fifty miles northeast of Memphis in Brownsville, Tennessee, Clay Evans was the fourth of nine children. His parents, Henry and Estanauly Evans, were natives of Brownsville, located in Haywood County, in the Delta Region of western Tennessee. In that county, where the Hatchie River runs straight through Brownsville, farming ruled supreme. In 1923, the fertile soil in Haywood County yielded a high level of crop diversification, with cotton, corn, fruit, grass, and livestock being the county's most important agricultural products.[5]

During the early 1920s, sharecroppers provided a plentiful supply of cheap labor in the region. Henry and Estanauly had both come from sharecropping families. Like countless African American southerners, Henry and Estanauly spent their childhoods enslaved in what scholar Jennifer Searcy refers to as the "endless cycle of financial rigging orchestrated by white landowners" achieved through the sharecropping system.[6] Within this system, financial stability became virtually impossible for African American southerners.[7] And certainly the threat of racial violence always hung in the atmosphere to discourage people from daring to challenge white-imposed social, economic, and legal restrictions. The logic was simple, as one former plantation owner explained: "Teach the Negro that if he goes to work, keeps his place, and behaves himself, he will be protected by our white laws."[8] Plantation owners passed down this culturally transmitted disease from the nineteenth to the early twentieth century. Like his grandparents and parents before him,

Clay Evans spent his childhood in this terrifying and unjust crucible of racial violence and oppression.

Most African American sharecropping families in Brownsville, Tennessee, during the early 1920s lived in housing on their employers' properties. The Evans family lived in a small, aging shack-like structure. Uninsulated wooden walls rested underneath a tin roof riddled with holes. Legions of gaps between the roof and the walls accented the ceiling. At night Evans often gazed out at the sky through these openings. "I looked up at night, and I could see the stars." During stormy weather, each gap, hole, and crack allowed tiny rivers of water to pour into the house. "Many times, we had to move the bed at night when it was raining," Evans recalled, chuckling. The battered linoleum floor resembled the roof. Small spaces in the floor revealed the family's chicken coop underneath the house.

Despite the structural imperfections of their house, the Evans family took much pride in presenting it in as dignified a manner as possible. The neatness of the always-swept porch, the shine of uncurtained windows, and artful placement of marigolds and day lilies along the home's unpaved walk, author Dorothy June Rose states, gave the Evans home "an air of dignity that even the blatant signs of abject poverty could not squelch." This quiet dignity reflected not only the physical appearance of the house but also the inner strength of the family residing within the home. Neighbors felt something special about the Evans family. Many in Brownsville's black sharecropping community often shared their personal joys and pains with Henry and Estanauly.

Since many who labored in the fields passed by the Evanses' home each day, it became a natural meeting place. Here men would meet their wives and children and enjoy a leisurely walk home to a meal already waiting. Rose stated, "And yet, even if it had not been so convenient, the cheerful greeting, the quiet encouragement always to be found in the Evans' home, would have made it a focal point in any setting."[9]

The Evanses' home had a small fireplace. However, its size did not diminish its importance. "In the wintertime, you'd make the fire at night, but you brought in a lot of wood in the evening to put on the fire until you go to bed. And you'd make it so that it wouldn't go all the way out. And in the morning, you'd stir up the ashes, and that kind of warmed the house." The family couldn't afford proper insulation or wallpaper. Instead, family members pasted newspapers on the walls to block cold winds from entering uninvited. "That's how poor we were," Evans explained. Family meals were cooked on a wood stove. "Those were really hard times." For baths, water was heated on the stove and then poured into a single bathtub. "Sometimes two or three people bathed in the same tub, not just in the same tub but in the same water," Evans recalled. "But when they got down to the second or third baths, there wasn't nothing but mud. We've come a long way."

Sleeping arrangements became particularly challenging as Evans and his nine brothers and sisters grew older. At bedtime, he and his siblings all crammed as many as they could into the same bed. "We slept three and four in the bed, two at the head and two at the feet." Those who didn't make it into the bed on a given night slept on the floor. Looking back on those experiences, Evans's brother Pharis said those cramped conditions strengthened the bonds between siblings:

> We had to be close to each other. We had no choice. I slept in the same bed that my brother Clay slept in and my brother Joe slept in the same bed. Sometimes there were more than two that slept in that bed. There are things that we had to do to be close to each other. And because of that when we left Brownsville we carried it with us. It was my brother Joe that took my sister Lou Della in when we got to Chicago. It was our brother Clay that opened the door and took me in.[10]

The Evans home had neither electricity nor running water. On the way home from school, the Evans children often stopped to pump water from a nearby well. "And sometimes that was infested with frogs," Evans remembered. His sister Lou Della also recalled those difficult days. "You know how to appreciate things now," she said. "Stuff you didn't have, now you have. It was hard. . . . We didn't have anything. We used each other's clothes. If they had some food left, you'd get their food, what they had left." It was a difficult life. Recalling those childhood days was painful for Evans and his siblings. "It has been a struggle the whole way," Lou Della recalled.

Usually only one black sharecropping family worked per white farm in Brownsville. White farmers required the children to begin working the fields as soon as they turned ten. Mothers were often forced to take their newborn infants with them into the fields each day. Estanauly held her younger children while she worked. When necessary, her older children relieved her and watched their younger siblings. "That's how women back then could have a dozen children. . . . They'd make the oldest take care of the little ones," Evans said. Henry and Estanauly taught their children to take care of each other. "So my older sister, she was like my mamma, 'cause she had to take care of me," Evans explained. His memories of those times are of grueling and relentless labor. Evans's chores were endless. He helped harvest corn, cotton, and peas. He fed hogs, milked cows, pulled cotton, dug trenches. "You get up with the sun, and you work until the sun goes down." Being a sickly child, Clay found the toil of sharecropping especially difficult. In fact, some of his younger siblings were better able to handle the rigors of farm labor. "I was looked down upon," Evans recalled.

The sharecropper's life was painfully monotonous. The Evans family arose each day before sunrise, usually shortly after 4:00 a.m. They ate breakfast. Then they walked to the fields to work. The backbreaking labor was unceasing. The sun was unrelenting. The Evans family labored nonstop except for brief rests during dinner and supper. The women got even less rest than the men. The Evans women left the fields early to prepare the family meals. "They'd go in the fields and work. And half an hour before dinnertime, they'd somehow come home to fix dinner and then go back to the fields," Evans recalled. "How women could double up like that, I don't know, but they did it." After dinner, around 1:00 p.m., the whole family, men and women, marched back to the fields, where they toiled under the hot sun until supper, usually around 6:00 p.m. but often later. At sunset, the family returned home, exhausted from their labors, only to get a few hours of sleep before waking up to perform the same ritual all over again. "You didn't count by hours," Evans explained about a typical day working as a sharecropper. "Sun up to sun down. You got up with the sun. And many times, you couldn't quit when the sun went down." Family members pushed their bodies often past their limits. They were always anxious about the potential consequences awaiting them should they fail to meet their employer's quotas and profits. Evans's sister Lou Della remembered the stress of that environment. "I didn't like the hard work there, not at all," she recalled. "But I did it. I didn't have a choice. So you do what you got to do. I never could wait until the time I could leave, to get away, to experience some of the other parts of life."

Against their will, Estanauly and Henry Evans exposed their children to the brutal life of sharecropping. "They had no alternative," Evans explained. White farmers contracted with black families to work their lands. However, sharecropping was designed to make it impossible for African Americans to achieve social mobility. No matter how many crops black families harvested, the sharecropping system depended on the perpetuation of black poverty. The most common practice among white farmers was to compensate black families below the market value for their labor. Additionally, white farmers often demanded exorbitant fees for black families to acquire basic resources like food and medicine, or basic work materials like mules and farm equipment. White farmers often required their black employees to live in housing located on their farms. Farmers then charged high rental rates for these shabby dwellings. Making black families economically dependent on white farmers lessened the possibility African Americans could build enough wealth to become financially self-sufficient. "You're never paid out of debt," Evans explained about sharecropping. "I don't care how much you raise. You're never paid out. You always owe them something. It was rough. . . . It was slavery time."

Nick Salvatore paints a vivid portrait of the exploitative sharecropping economy in his account of the childhood of famed preacher Rev. C. L. Franklin in the Mississippi Delta. It is strikingly familiar to Evans's childhood in rural Tennessee. Franklin, born in 1915, would become the father of singer Aretha Franklin and one of Evans's close friends. Sharecroppers in Mississippi's Sunflower County relied on plantation stores to meet their needs between April, when the cotton was planted, and December, when all accounts were settled. However, prices were 10 to 25 percent higher in these stores. The annual rent for housing usually consumed half the value of crops harvested. And when sharecroppers brought their crops to the mill for processing, grading, and sale, the expenses they had incurred living on the farm during the year were deducted. Salvatore elaborates further:

"Given the 25 percent illiteracy rate among blacks and the near-total powerlessness before a determined white owner, few tenants finished any year with a profit. If they did, they were usually paid in credit redeemable only at plantation stores."[11] Like Franklin's family, Evans and his kin in Brownsville found themselves victims of the sharecropping system's scheme to trap successive generations of black southerners in virtually inescapable webs of economic oppression.

Tragically, the dehumanizing sharecropping culture often caused strain between parents and their children. Under intense pressure to meet their white employers' production quotas, and desperate to get out from underneath their oppressor's boot, some parents were often cold toward their children. Evans recalled how sharecropping affected his relationship with his father, Henry. When asked to describe the nature of his relationship with his father, Evans paused momentarily, completely motionless. Then, after a long silence, he finally shared:

> My father always expected us to do a day's work, which was amazing to me what he called a day's work, with plows that weren't good plows, horses and mules that were not good horses or mules. But not having proper equipment. And that was one lesson that I really learned. That if I had somebody doing something they ought to be given the proper tools to work with. How could we with the handle of the plow broke, plough hand dull . . . and expect a good day's work? So I always

used that as an example if I had secretaries I wanted them to have what it'd take to work with. If I had good musicians, given them good equipment, instruments to work with. Give the people what is necessary to really do a good job just if you expect a good job. "Why didn't you plow this?" I couldn't tell whether he understood the old ploughs that he gave me were dull and wouldn't stay in the ground. The mules were so slow.[12]

Probing his memory further, Evans recalled the often-tense dynamics that arose between his father and his brothers and himself. "He was pretty tough on us for doing a day's work. If an accident had happened, like we broke a plow point or something, we would get a whipping for it. Sometimes you would hit a rock or hit a root or something, and the plow would somewhat break. But you couldn't see what was in the ground. It was an accident. But you got a whipping for that." Despite his father's tough nature in the fields, Evans understood the heavy weight his father carried as the head of a family of sharecroppers. "He expected us to really produce because the white man was expecting him to produce."

Amid the unharmonious family dynamics sharecropping often created, Evans's mother made sure the melodies of prayer, hope, faith, and God rang more loudly. Estanauly was a woman of faith. She believed in her husband and children. But most importantly, she believed in a God who could do the impossible. Estanauly believed in a God who intervened in human affairs to set wrong things right, to liberate the oppressed. One of the ways Estanauly and Henry Evans believed God could liberate their family was through education. If their children could receive a quality education, they believed, then, with God's help, they could escape those seemingly impervious chains of inferiority that had been forged for black children from the moment of their birth in rural towns like Brownsville in the 1920s.

In Brownsville, black children did not attend school nine months out of the year. "We couldn't go to school. Crops had to be worked," Evans explained. However, black families created alternate avenues to educate their children. Schooling for children between first and eighth grades in Brownsville occurred between December and February, because there were no crops to plant or harvest during the winter months. "They always arranged schools at a time that you wasn't really needed on the farm." Children received education in a one-room schoolhouse, where first through eighth grades met together with two or three black teachers, usually committed parents dreaming of better lives for their children. Evans's mother never attended high school, but she served as a teacher for a time. When winter ended, children and their families went right back to working their white employers' farms. "The farm came first, as far as the boss man was concerned," Evans remembered. "He didn't care whether black folks got an education or not." In fact, one of the white farmers for whom the Evans family worked attempted to stop the family's efforts to advance the education of Evans's big sister, Gladys. "The boss man tried to get my parents not to send my older sister, Gladys, to school or to send her to college. But mamma was determined that Gladys would go on to get an education. So she went to Lane College in Jackson, Tennessee. She got a degree where she could teach," Evans said proudly.

Once children in Brownsville began attending high school, if they attended at all, they usually attended nine months out of the year. A family's decision to send children to high school meant that there would be one less pair of arms and legs to work the fields. And there was always the inevitable conflict that arose with white farmers who objected to losing a member of their workforce. In the early 1900s, many white southerners, particularly those in rural areas, believed schooling made African Americans unfit for work in a southern economy that depended on an unskilled black labor force. As scholar James R. Grossman argues, "Black southerners who wished to keep their children in school for nine months out of every year faced a task that was at best difficult and usually impossible."[13] Evans's parents were determined to secure a better future for their children. "My parents wanted us to have an education!" Evans said emphatically. Both his parents encouraged him to attend Brownsville's all-black Carver High School.

Evans had always struggled academically. "He really wasn't smart at all. . . . He had to do what he had to do to live and get along," his sister Lou Della recalled. "But extra stuff, smartness? No way!" Evans remembered those difficult years in school with a sense of humor, saying, "I never made more than a C; A is when I was absent; B is when I was bad." The humiliating oppression of sharecropping culture created in young Clay Evans intense feelings of inferiority, anxiety, and anger. The painful daily experiences of a black sharecropper's life traumatized him well into his teen years. By the time Evans was a teenager, his self-confidence had been damaged severely. The psychological effects of sharecropping had taken their toll. Evans turned inward. He became increasingly self-conscious, introverted, and withdrawn. Unfortunately, Evans's transition to the all-black Carver High School only intensified these feelings.

The Evans home was about ten miles from Carver High School. Given the family's limited resources, the only way Evans could attend school was if he stayed in town. Thankfully, the Evans family knew a woman named Mrs. Mark, who lived near the high school. Mrs. Mark agreed to rent Evans a room in her house. He would pay for his room and board by completing long lists of tasks, such as chopping wood. Though anxious about Clay living away from home for the first time, Evans's parents were excited about the arrangement. It would mean the beginning of a better life for their son. Evans's mother, the rock of the family, offered poignant words to her son on the eve of his departure for his great adventure to live with Mrs. Mark and begin his high school career:

And to think when you was a little boy we thought you was dumb. Not talkin' till you was almost three. And now you're goin' on to high school. It just goes to show the Lord has everythin' in His plan. It was the Lord who finally helped you find your voice. It was the Lord who somehow let us keep you in the grade school even when times was so bad we could have used another wages from the fields. But I always knew you wasn't meant to be no field hand. Somehow I just knew the Lord wanted you for another reason. Now I know I was right.[14]

Evans's mother reminded him of the important role his faith would play in the journey that lay ahead. The Evans family was a church family, a faithful family, and a praying family. And as a praying woman, Evans's mother would make sure her son did not forget where he came from. She encouraged her son further, saying, "We raised you right, boy. Now you just keep to prayin' and hard work. We'll all be prayin' for you here, too. Whatever it takes, it'll be worth it in the end. You're the Lord's man, Clay. He is goin' to see you through."[15]

It was 1941, and sixteen-year-old Clay Evans was full of confidence, pride, and excitement that night before he began high school. But the journey would prove more difficult than he imagined. There were legions of unforeseen challenges. Hosts of disappointments were lying in wait.

High school proved difficult for young Clay Evans. He wasn't a strong student. How could he be? He was so busy during the day, doing endless chores for Mrs. Mark. As soon as school ended each day, Mrs. Mark consumed Evans's time with work like chopping wood, running personal errands, cleaning the house, and cutting the grass. But she remained an unsatisfied taskmaster. She didn't let a day pass without reminding Clay how fortunate he was to be allowed to live in her home. Given Mrs. Mark's grueling expectations, Evans could only study late at night. Evans strained himself for his C grades.

Mrs. Mark wasn't the only challenging personality Clay faced during high school. His classmates also were formidable. Black students living in town often looked down on country kids like Evans. He was the son of a poor sharecropping family who was a less-than-average student with no athletic interest or prowess. Evans became a regular target for bullies' embarrassing jokes. Worse yet, unlike many of his classmates, Evans had no spending money. Evans recalled those difficult moments in high school: "Maybe mamma's wrong. Maybe the Lord don't have nothin' special in store for me. Maybe I should have just stayed on the farm and done my share like the rest."[16]

There were days when Evans packed his things and began making his way back to his parents' home. But his family's faith in him prevented him from leaving each time. Their optimism in his future always called him back to face his bad grades and failed high school popularity. Perhaps it was the image of seeing the excitement in his mother's eyes as she made her way to town each Sunday in the family's rickety wagon to bring sweet treats, homemade jam, fresh bread, or vegetables from the family garden to augment Mrs. Mark's sparse meals.[17]

Evans vowed to not let his insecurities or limitations slow his progress. He had much to overcome, but the biggest barrier standing in Evans's path was not sharecropping, racist farmers, high school bullies, or poverty; it was accepting and loving himself. "Because I always felt inferior. And my looks, my mental capacity. . . . I could never make good grades. And when I was a youngster, I looked terrible. There wasn't a spot on my face where I didn't have pimples. Not a spot on my face. You may never think so today, but when it came to competing with others, . . . I had to work on that, even after I got grown and accepted the ministry."

Evans's low self-esteem as a teenager had negative effects on his social life, especially with girls. The girls his age didn't find him attractive. "During my teenage years I couldn't get a girl. And that can kind of hurt you. All the other boys could get girls. But I couldn't. They rejected me." His high school years weren't filled with scores of memories attending school dances with girls or hanging out socially after school. In fact, by the age of twenty, Clay Evans had never been on a date![18] Much later, looking back on those days, Evans laughed as he recalled the times when, after he achieved success later in life, he returned to Brownsville, full of confidence, to strut in the presence of the girls who had rejected him for sport. "When I got grown and got to Chicago and was able to do pretty good I got a car and I went back down there (to Brownsville). . . . See what you rejected!"

When Evans began his journey at Carver High School in 1941, World War II had just erupted. Slowly, the number of boys in grades higher than Evans began to dwindle, as those of draft age were summoned overseas. Evans's parents had always taught him to detest war, violence, and killing. But he found great pride in the idea of serving the country and returning home a hero. Maybe if he were a war hero, his peers would look at him differently. Maybe enlisting might help him to overcome his insecurities. When young Clay Evans told his parents about his plans to enlist, a stern reaction followed. It was one of the few times he remembered his mother shouting at him: "We didn't work for your education all these years only to have you blown up and buried on the other side of the ocean. You're the Lord's man, Clay. I've know'd it from the day you were born. He has a mission for you and I'll see you fulfill it if it's the last thin' I do."[19]

Evans remained adamant about enlisting. But each year, the call to serve never came. In 1945, as a senior in high school and almost twenty-one years old, Clay Evans was one of just three males remaining in his class. It didn't make any sense. He was strong. He was fit. He was classified as 1-A. For the first time, Evans began to consider more seriously the possible providence in his mother's visions for his life. "Maybe mama's right. Maybe there is somethin' special the Lord wants me to do."[20]

NOTES

1. Dorothy June Rose, *From Plough Handle to Pulpit: The Life Story of Rev. Clay Evans, a Man with a Mission* (Warminster, PA: Neibauer, 1981), 9.

2. Rose, *From Plough Handle to Pulpit*, 8.

3. Rose, *From Plough Handle to Pulpit*, 8–9.

4. Rose, *From Plough Handle to Pulpit*, 10.

5. Emma Nunn, "Haywood County," *The Tennessee Encyclopedia of History and Culture*, updated 2017, http://tinyurl.com/ybb6hpcl.

6. Jennifer Searcy, "The Voice of the Negro: African American Radio, WVON, and the Struggle for Civil Rights in Chicago" (PhD diss., Loyola University, 2003), p. 27, paper 688, http://tinyurl.com/y7gpcxya.

7. James R. Grossman, *Land of Hope: Chicago, Black Southerners, and the Great Migration* (Chicago: University of Chicago Press, 1989), 42.

8. Leon Litwack, *Been in the Storm So Long: The Aftermath of Slavery* (New York: Knopf, 1979), 366.

9. Rose, *From Plough Handle to Pulpit*, 7–8.

10. Rev. Pharis Evans, interview by the author, 2012, Fellowship Missionary Baptist Church, Chicago.

11. Nick Salvatore, *Singing in a Strange Land: C. L. Franklin, the Black Church, and the Transformation of America* (Urbana: University of Illinois Press, 2006), 11.

12. Rev. Clay Evans, interview by the author, 2012, Chicago, Rev. Clay Evans's home.

13. Grossman, *Land of Hope*, 249.

14. Rose, *From Plough Handle to Pulpit*, 12.

15. Rose, *From Plough Handle to Pulpit*, 13.

16. Rose, *From Plough Handle to Pulpit*, 13–14.

17. Rose, *From Plough Handle to Pulpit*, 14.

18. Rose, *From Plough Handle to Pulpit*, 13–14.

19. Rose, *From Plough Handle to Pulpit*, 15.

20. Rose, *From Plough Handle to Pulpit*, 15.

2

EAR ALL THE WAY DOWN

The principles that I learned from my mother at home and at church have helped to carry me through life.

—Rev. Clay Evans (2013)

On Sunday nights we would get the broadcast from Memphis. We were about fifty miles from Memphis. With the radio that we had at that time you had to put your ear all the way down.

—Lou Della Evans-Reid (2011)

BETWEEN 1935 AND 1945—In Brownsville during Clay Evans's childhood, as in many rural towns throughout the South in the early 1900s, the ever-hovering shadow of racial violence terrorized the town. Evans's voice gets softer, his eyes lower, and his sentences shorter whenever he talks about those early years. The memories are almost too painful to speak aloud. Those unhappy, traumatic early years haunt him even today. However, after he reflected silently, he found the strength to talk about those harsh childhood experiences: "We knew that we were black and subject to white people. They made all the laws." As Evans searched for more words, his struggle within became visible—his blank expression, his passive posture, his eyes welling with tears.

This biographer felt reluctant asking Evans to bare his childhood scars through testimony, even given the possibility that exposing such wounds would be therapeutic. Interviewing Evans about his childhood raised the question of whether it was humane, whether it was worth the stress and strain it created for Evans. Witnessing that moment when Evans answered questions about his early years—that agonizing moment when his body visually morphed from a confident elder into a traumatized youth, when his still-vibrant voice dwindled to a whisper, when this seasoned, self-assured professional began to search anxiously for psychological sanctuary and exit, that complicated and strange moment when Clay Evans transfigured from a famous, powerful black preacher into a poor black sharecropper and back again—made this biographer question the civility of this project.

African Americans in Brownsville were left with limited financial and political means to confront discrimination directly, so they learned more indirect strategies of resistance. Home and church were the primary places where Evans, like other black sharecroppers, learned such survival tactics. Evans explained, "Like most black folks in the

South, you learn how to cope with whatever your circumstances are. And black folks learned how to deal and get along with white folks."

Evans's parents served as his first instructors in the art of subverting racism creatively. For instance, Estanauly demonstrated for Evans how one could indirectly confront economic discrimination through savvy entrepreneurial wits. She tended a garden next to the family's home. There she grew a variety of vegetables, including okra, corn, and lima beans. White farmers forbade their black employees from claiming ownership of the crops harvested from the farms on which they worked. But crops grown in small black family gardens belonged to those who tended them. Thus, Estanauly leveraged her skill in gardening to create a bunker economy outside the sharecropping economy that generated extra income for her family:

> My mother was a hard worker and she really supported the family because she had a garden and she used to peddle vegetables in town. Knocking on the white peoples' doors get them to buy a gallon of this, or two ears of corn or whatnot. She really supported the family out of her garden because whatever was raised in the field belongs to the white folks whose farm we lived on. But they could not claim that little garden.[1]

Lou Della, Evans's sister, recalled how her mother's business savvy provided an alternate revenue stream for the family and inspired an entrepreneurial spirit among the

Evans children: "That's how she helped us to get clothes. . . . And so you can make it, and we did make it. That was the beginning of us, the growth that we had, mentally, physically, spiritually. We got our growth there."

Evans's father, Henry, also taught Evans and his siblings how to maneuver within and in spite of racist systems. Henry's curriculum in resistance involved a shrewd combination of humility and boldness. "He would say, 'Get off the sidewalk when white people walk by' or say 'Yes, sir' and 'Yes, ma'am.'" Certainly, if his goal was achieving a measure of safety or self-preservation, Henry knew not to challenge white folks directly. However, he also practiced indirect ways of challenging whites. "My father mortgaged a property twice," Evans said, laughing. "He mortgaged something on the farm, one white man over here and another over there." However, somehow one or both of the parties learned the truth, and his father's plan backfired. Henry immediately began making plans to leave Brownsville, because he was certain violent retaliation would follow. "So my daddy got ready to leave his family, because he didn't want to get hung. He started devising a way to get away from Brownsville, because those white folks were going to get him. He mortgaged the same property to two different people," Evans repeated, laughing again, louder this time. As it turned out, his father didn't leave Brownsville. But Evans exclaimed, "He was in trouble, man, big trouble!"

Evans's parents taught him to preserve his dignity and to celebrate the beauty of black lives in the face of racist, unjust, and inhumane people and institutions. He learned from Henry and Estanauly that even in a racist society, he could forge a new path toward self-determination, self-affirmation, self-assuredness, and independence. Those early lessons at home taught Evans how to execute creative leadership during dark and difficult times. Those lessons would serve him well in the years ahead, when he would be responsible for teaching racially oppressed communities how to survive similarly dark and difficult times in Chicago.

While Evans's parents imparted valuable lessons in the home, church became another place where Evans gained a stunning arsenal of philosophical, theological, and practical tools for navigating life. Church anchored the Evans family. It offered the second wind family members needed to return to the suffocating sharecropping fields on Monday morning. Sunday was the only day black sharecropping families in Brownsville had off from their labors. The Evans family attended church regularly for much-needed inspiration and the strength to face the coming week. "I think religion played a great part in helping people to kind of survive during all of this," Evans said. "That's why many of the old spirituals . . . gave them a little more hope."

The Evans family adored religious music. On Sunday nights after spending the morning at church, the family often gathered in the home to sing. Lou Della remembered those family moments fondly: "We all loved to sing. My mom had a piano. So that was our thing. On Sunday nights, you had nowhere to go. So I would play the piano, and my dad and my mom and the rest of us would sing."

Evans's siblings never witnessed Evans singing much as

a boy. But he radiated an obvious fascination with both music and singing. All his family members knew Clay loved *hearing* singing! On Sunday evenings, Lou Della often saw her brother crouched beside the family radio, listening to broadcasts airing church services from Memphis and Chicago:

> I just knew that Clay loved singing. That thing was more with him than anything else. On Sunday nights we would get the broadcast from Memphis. We were about fifty miles from Memphis. With the radio that we had and at that time you had to put your ear all the way down and a lot of Sunday nights I could see him with his ear listening to Rev. [William Herbert] Brewster who was one of the main pastors down in Memphis, listening to their broadcast.[2] And even late at night, at eleven or twelve o'clock at night, we could pick up First Church of Deliverance [in Chicago], but you had to put both ears all the way down, coming all the way from Chicago so late at night we could get through but you could hardly hear it. So as you look back you could see his yearning and desire, longing to want to hear, and go further, and get into the Gospel, into the Word, into songs, or whatever he was doing. You could tell it, as I look back, I could see it then.[3]

This ritual of radio listening was common among African American southerners in the early part of the twentieth century. For many poor blacks in the South, radio became an affordable way of having experiences with different people and places that racism and poverty often prevented. While radio was not the first technological innovation to revolutionize mass communication, the speed and scale of communication that radio allowed was not possible in previous generations.[4] Whether used as an entertainment or information medium, radio afforded African Americans unprecedented mobility. It brought them to new worlds, and brought new worlds to them. By 1940, 83 percent of Americans owned a radio.[5] Given the unprecedented mobility radio afforded listeners, it makes sense why African Americans such as Clay Evans would place such importance on radio listening in the home. Religious radio in particular offered Evans immediate escape, as it transported him beyond the physical and psychological boundaries containing him in Brownsville. The faint, almost inaudible radio broadcasts of singing and preaching from Memphis and Chicago ricocheted between Evans's ears while his imagination sailed on ephemeral waves toward more hopeful shores.

The Evans family attended Woodlawn Missionary Baptist Church. Woodlawn, Evans boasted, was "the most outstanding country church in that community." Rev. Hardin Smith established the church in 1866. Smith had learned to read and write from his former slave owner's wife, who read the Bible to him. At age sixteen, Smith was allowed to preach as a slave preacher to a select group of slaves during night services at the white Woodlawn Baptist Church in

Nutbush. But Smith secretly preached and taught congregations of slaves to read and write near the Hatchie River in Brownsville. In 1866, supported by the Baptist Home Missionary Board of New York City, Smith, along with the Freedmen's Bureau and white residents of Nutbush, established Woodlawn Colored Baptist Church, later called Woodlawn Missionary Baptist Church, where Smith remained pastor for the next fifty-six years.

Smith was a master community organizer. Through his leadership, members of the Woodlawn Missionary Baptist Church promoted education and established schools throughout Haywood and Shelby Counties. In 1867, Smith and five others founded the first school for freed slaves, the Freedmen's School of Brownsville, which is now Carver High School, where Evans attended high school.[6] Under Smith's leadership, Woodlawn Missionary Baptist Church gathered and organized black musicians and singers and promoted local artists to perform in venues throughout and well beyond Haywood County. Many of these performers were able to move easily between sacred music and the blues and jazz. Haywood County and Woodlawn Baptist Church gave the world such greats as Sleepy John Estes, the Bootsie Whitelow String Band, singer/actor Meshach Taylor, Tina Turner, and gospel recording artist Clay Evans.[7]

The physical location of Woodlawn Missionary Baptist Church was Woodlawn Road, south of TN 19 (now Tina Turner Highway) in Nutbush, Tennessee. The church was a drawing card for many inspiring young pastors. In the 1930s, when Evans was in elementary school, Woodlawn had about two hundred members. "Back then, that was very good," Evans boasted about the church's membership. "We had many people who wanted to pastor Woodlawn because they felt it was prosperous, famous." And they were right.

Rev. William T. Grafton was pastor during all of Evans's elementary and some of his high school years between 1934 and 1942.[8] Grafton often encouraged church members to remain hopeful in the face of the racism swirling around them. The worship culture at Woodlawn was rather reserved. While some participated in the call-and-response tradition of African American worship, the majority of the congregation was more introspective during worship services. Grafton's preaching style, however, was more animated. He often ended his sermons chanting in carefully timed, rhythmic, and musical intonations fused with intense emotion. It was Grafton who first introduced Evans to the celebrated preaching tradition of African American whooping.[9] "Grafton had all the emotional side that we lack. I got some of mine from him," Evans proudly attested.

The Evans family attended church every Sunday. His mother played the piano during worship services. "My mother was very religious." His father wasn't a particularly religious man, but he still attended church with the family. "My father was an ordinary man." It was at Woodlawn that Evans learned the basic teachings of Christianity. There he made his first public profession of faith in Jesus Christ. He remembers the day fondly. The church was hosting its annual revival the fourth week in August 1935. The week-long revival began on Monday and ended on Friday.

Throughout the week, congregation members listened to Reverend Grafton preach passionately. Any worshippers who felt they had heard from the Holy Spirit made their way to the mourner's bench at the end of the sermon, when Reverend Grafton invited people to accept Christ. There, on the mourner's bench, crying and repentant sinners confessed their faith in Jesus and vowed to live new and transformed lives. Each evening during the revival, Evans watched people dedicate their lives to Jesus Christ. On the Sunday afternoon after the revival, at the end of Grafton's sermon, young Clay Evans rose to his feet and made his way to the mourner's bench to accept Jesus as his personal savior. "That was the day that I confessed my hope in Christ. . . . There was no lightening flash, no thunder crash." There was no dramatic or discernable prick of the Holy Spirit.

For as long as Evans could remember, his family and fellow church members had talked to him about Jesus Christ. So by the time he made his way to the mourner's bench that hot summer Sunday in August 1935, Evans had already been persuaded about Christianity's claim about Jesus's identity as God's son: "At home I was taught to say my prayers before I was saved, so to speak. 'Now I lay me down to sleep.' . . . I wasn't even a Christian then, but Mama taught me that . . . so therefore when I was offered Christ as my savior during the revival, I could accept it. I didn't have to fall out on the floor or roll on the floor."[10] In other words, Evans's profession of Jesus Christ that Sunday was the public confirmation of a prior inward decision. "Back then, you usually waited until revival time," Evans explained, which was the protocol many people observed when joining Woodlawn Missionary Baptist Church.

Evans credited his mother and his experiences at Woodlawn with giving him values that guided him during his life outside Brownsville. "The principles that I learned from my mother at home and at church have helped to carry me through life." A devout woman, Estanauly taught her children life lessons rooted in biblical principles, particularly the teachings of Jesus. "The boys learned how to respect their mother and their sisters," Evans recalled. "And any boy that don't respect their mother or his sister won't make a good husband. Any girl that won't respect her daddy and her brother won't make a good wife. It begins at home. . . . If you've got a good husband, it's because he learned how to respect his mother and his sister, the females in his family. If he didn't respect them, he ain't gonna respect you," Evans counseled.

Evans is grateful for the wealth of religious values, rituals, practices, and beliefs he learned in home and in church. This home and church-grown spiritual formation, he testified, has guided, sustained, and informed him in every season of his personal and professional life. "So this kind of thing comes from the home and the church," he insisted. Lou Della agreed that the church had a central role in the Evans family. She declared:

We had no choice. We went to church. Church was another thing we looked forward to going on Sunday. At least we got a rest day [from working the fields]. We enjoyed the members there. That's where we got our start. We had to go to church. I had to sing in the choir. My mother gave me music and then she'd send me to a music teacher. And I started playing [the piano] for the church. So I had a taste of church. Had a taste of singing. Had a taste of working. That was deep down within. You can't help that taste. That was your desire. Had a hunger and thirst.[11]

During those early years at Woodlawn Missionary Baptist Church, Evans learned what it meant for a person of faith to have integrity. "Religion plays an important part of a person's character," he said. "It molds you, gets you in a certain pattern." The church provided Evans with a model for ethical leadership. "It had a lot to do with my conduct, with my thinking about things. Therefore, I never was wild . . . I never was crazy about parties and drinking. I used to try to dance a little, but my feet were too flat to dance. It also had to do with my choice of a woman to marry. I tried to find someone very much like my mother." It was the church's teachings and his mother's piety that taught him the importance of integrity. "It navigates you through life," he said.

In 1942, when Evans was seventeen, Reverend Grafton left Woodlawn. Historical accounts of the circumstances of Grafton's departure are limited. However, Evans's testimony suggests congregation members may have voted Grafton out or white pressure may have forced him out. The turnover rate for pastors at Woodlawn was high. "My church there never kept a pastor more than six years," Evans recalled. This was primarily because many of the church's members worked the land as sharecroppers. They were bound to the land in a very real way. Thus, if a conflict ever arose between the pastor and church members, the pastor usually lost.

Regardless of the circumstances surrounding Rev. W. T. Grafton's departure from Woodlawn, his ministry made a lasting impression on Evans. In particular, Evans learned from Grafton that one of the primary roles of a Christian pastor is to offer a congregation vision. The pastor's vocation, Evans admonished, involves the unique task of discerning the liberating ways forward amid the painful, joyful, and ambiguous experiences of daily life. Reflecting on the circumstances under which Reverend Grafton left Woodlawn Missionary Baptist Church, Evans insisted:

> Boards cannot lead a church. And they want to make all the rules and want to minister like a corporation. But the church is more than an organization; it's an organism. And many of the black churches now are leaning toward corporations. . . . Moses had to be a leader. Jesus had disciples to help. Without a vision, the people perish. It's hard for a trustee board or a deacon board to have a vision. . . . I know many think that a board is supposed to. . . . That's good for a corporation. But no board can lead a church. I don't care what you name the board. It takes a shepherd, a leader, and a pastor, to lead, to have vision.

Whatever led to Reverend Grafton leaving Wood-lawn—whether pressures put upon members from their white employers, hostilities his preaching may have pro-voked, or Grafton's own painful experiences with race in Brownsville—memories of the challenges of life in Brownsville continue to haunt Evans. "We've gone through some horrible pain, but we're still here" Evans resolved.

Still, the traumatic circumstances Evans experienced as a teenager have never fully vanished from his mind. They're ghosts in his memory he can conjure at will. For instance, Evans recalled the time when he was in grade school and befriended a white boy from a poor family. Poverty alien-ated this boy from his wealthier white peers. "He needed some fellowship, so he tried to make friends with black boys." Evans and his friends welcomed the boy into their social circle. They played, laughed, and when time permit-ted, embarked upon exciting adventures exploring forests, rivers, and the Haywood County countryside. However, the bonds of friendship soon broke. While not offering specific details about the incident, Evans recalled the boy attempted to assert some perceived superiority over his black friends. "One day he decided to show his whiteness, his superior-ity," Evans remembered. Angered by the sense of betrayal, Evans said, "I went upside his head." He actually struck the boy! Because both the Evans family and his white friend's family were poor, Evans explained, the incident never erupted in violent retaliation from the boy's parents. Their shared poverty seemed to lessen—though not eradi-cate—the tension. However, the incident taught Evans the painful lesson that even whites as poor as black sharecroppers were not immune to inheriting gangrenous stains of the culturally transmitted disease of racism.

Evans recounted another haunting ghost of his youth. "I will never forget, on a Sunday evening, me and my friend were walking on the street. An old white man approached, walking with a cane. He told us, 'Boy, any time you see a white man, you ain't supposed to be on the sidewalk!'" The incident was a painful reminder that not even black youth were protected from prejudice in Brownsville. "Brownsville was the most segregated little town you could find anywhere!" Evans exclaimed. In fact, at the time, Brownsville police officers had no reservations about abusing their power to harass African Americans. "Either you were driving too slow, or you were speeding," Evans recalled. "And you didn't dispute that."

Every day in Brownsville, African Americans endured painful reminders of their inferior social status. "Those white folks were so mean to black folks there." Tragically, some whites perpetrated worse crimes than verbal abuse or racial profiling. On June 20, 1940, Elbert Williams, a thirty-one-year old Laundromat owner and charter member of an NAACP chapter in Brownsville, was murdered. According to an article on National Public Radio's website, Williams was part of a group of black professionals and business owners who had formed an NAACP chapter in Haywood County to register African American voters.[12] However, whites terrorized the new NAACP officers with violence and burned some of their houses. Some of the NAACP members fled the city for their lives. Elbert Williams agreed that he would host a chapter meeting at his home. But before he could host that meeting, police took him from his home late at night and placed him in jail.[13] Three days later, on June 23, Williams's body was found in the Hatchie River just a few minutes' drive from Brownsville. A log was tied to his body. When Williams's wife, Annie, identified her husband's body, she described what looked like two bullet holes in his chest.[14] A local grand jury decided that Williams had died by "foul violence at the hands of parties unknown." Williams is believed to have been the first known member of the NAACP to be killed for his work in civil rights.[15] And while convictions have never been made for Williams's murder, retired attorney Jim Emison has been investigating the case in hopes of finding evidence that might lead to discovering who murdered Williams.[16] In Memphis, US Attorney Edward Stanton has stated his office is trying to determine if there is enough information to reopen the case.[17]

By the time he turned twenty-one, Evans decided it was time for him to move on from Brownsville. "I knew I had to leave Brownsville, because [of] all the racism. . . . My opportunities were limited. I needed to get out of there." Evans wasn't finished with high school, but he knew there was no future for him in Brownsville. It was time to venture to a new land and toward a new life. And he wasn't alone. Waves of African Americans from all over the South had already moved to northern industrial cities in search of greater opportunities. This great migration involved many African Americans uprooting their entire families from the South in hopes of escaping the physical, psychological, and economic brutality of southern life. Listening to his family's radio, Evans heard the vibrancy, the resiliency, and the possibility of black lives in these other cities. He heard this energy calling him on a journey to find more abundant life. With his ear all the way down, Evans heard God call him north, to Chicago, to a land where waves of his black southern kin had already cascaded. With his ear all the way down, Evans decided to liberate his body from the painful boundaries of Brownsville. His mind had left years earlier, riding radio waves toward bright dreams in far-off lands. With his ear all the way down, Evans prepared to venture north toward a divine calling, to the land where America, and the world, would come to know his name.

NOTES

1. Rev. Clay Evans, interview by the author, 2012, Chicago.

2. Rev. William Herbert Brewster Sr. (1897–1987) was the oldest of eight siblings born to sharecropper parents (William and Callie Polk Brewster) on a farm near Somerville, Tennessee. He went to Memphis Howe Collegiate Institute and eventually graduated from Roger Williams University in Nashville, in 1922. When prohibited by Memphis authorities from establishing an African American seminary in Memphis, he founded the Brewster Theological Clinic, which had sites throughout the United States. Brewster was pastor of the East Trigg Baptist Church in

Memphis for fifty years. As editor of the *Beacon Light in Forest City*, which was the only newspaper between Memphis and Little Rock aimed at black audiences, and broadcasting on WDIA, the nation's first radio station with an all-black format, Brewster had a far-reaching influence as a writer, educator, and preacher. However, he is perhaps remembered best as a gospel music composer, especially between 1945 and 1960. He published over two hundred songs that included "I'm Leaning and Depending on the Lord" (1939), "Move on Up a Little Higher" (1941), and "Surely, God Is Able" (1947). These last two songs were the first black gospel recordings to sell over a million copies. "Peace Be Still" and "Let Us Go Back to the Old Landmark" (1949) were widely popular. Much of his music was heard and popularized by singers such as Mahalia Jackson, Clara Ward, Queen C. Anderson, and the Brewster Ensemble. Linda T. Wynn, "William Herbert Brewster Sr. (1897–1987)," *The Tennessee Encyclopedia of History and Culture*, January 1, 2010, http://tinyurl.com/ycjplo7r.

3. Lou Della Evans-Reid, interview by the author, 2012, Fellowship Missionary Baptist Church, Chicago. For the significance of Rev. Clarence Cobbs and First Church of Deliverance, see Wallace D. Best, *Passionately Human, No Less Divine: Religion and Culture in Black Chicago, 1915–1952* (Princeton: Princeton University Press, 2005), 40–43.

4. For more on the cultural significance of radio, see Susan J. Douglas, *Listening In: Radio and the American Imagination* (New York: Times Books, 1999).

5. Barbara Savage, *Broadcasting Freedom: Radio, War, and the Politics of*

Radio, 1938–1948 (Chapel Hill: University of North Carolina Press, 1999), 6.

6. Sharon Norris, "Hardin Smith," *The Tennessee Encyclopedia of History and Culture*, February 28, 2011, http://tinyurl.com/y9g57avp.

7. See, Sharon Norris, "Historic Woodlawn Baptist Church," in *Haywood County Tennessee*, Black America Series (Charleston, SC: Arcadia, 2000), 71–86.

8. Rev. William T. Grafton was born in Mississippi about 1904. At the time of the 1940 census, he was thirty-six years old. He completed one year of college. US Federal Census, 1940, www.ancestry.com. A portrait of Grafton appears in Norris, *Haywood County Tennessee*, 73.

9. For more information on the history, style, and dynamics of the African American preaching tradition of whooping, see Martha Simmons. "Whooping: The Musicality of African American Preaching Past and Present," in *Preaching with Sacred Fire: An Anthology of African American Sermons, 1750 to the Present*, ed. Martha Simmons and Frank A. Thomas (New York: W. W. Norton, 2010), 864–84.

10. Rev. Clay Evans, interview.

11. Lou Della Evans-Reid, interview.

12. Debbie Elliott, "Tennessee Community Pushes to Reopen 'Civil Rights Hero' Cold Case," *All Things Considered*, July 16, 2015, http://tinyurl.com/yc9sjzxh.

13. Jim Emison, "Williams, Elbert (1908–1940)," *Online Encyclopedia of*

Significant People and Places in African American History, BlackPast.org, http://tinyurl.com/y9jhnh2g.

14. Elliott, "Tennessee Community Pushes."

15. Emison, "Williams, Elbert."

16. Catherine Arnold, "Cold Case: Jim Emison, BA'65, Is Determined to Solve a 75-Year-Old Hate Crime and Bring Justice to Tragedy," *Vanderbilt Magazine*, February 29, 2016, http://tinyurl.com/ yavtl5dq. Emison is utilizing modern forensic science personnel to find Williams's body, which could be in one of eleven unmarked graves researchers with the University of Tennessee Forensic Anthropology Department have previously found. Emison believes that if Williams's body is found and bullets are recovered, it might be possible to find the gun that killed him.

17. Elliott, "Tennessee Community Pushes."

3

WALK IN JERUSALEM

"You wouldn't think I've been through what I've been through"

—Rev. Clay Evans

THE YEAR WAS 1945—Like young Richard Wright, Clay Evans dreamed of living in Chicago. In both men's imaginations, the city was a New Jerusalem—a land of opportunity, a place of new beginnings, a hallowed metropolis for realizing dreams. According to historian Timuel Black, the benefit of shared interests among the southern blacks who found themselves confined to Chicago's South Side was part of the allure that drew other migrants to the city. "There was a feeling of kinship," Black said about the African Americans who arrived during the massive northern migration of black southerners in the generation after Reconstruction. "We knew we were poor, but we were not depressed," Black recalled. "We could see a future, and we saw the possibilities in the personalities [of black professionals]."[1]

For many African Americans living in the South during

the 1940s, the hopeful possibilities radiating from the Midwest metropolis were like bright beacons hailing those brave enough to make the journey north. The stories that southern migrants told visitors from the South or friends and family still living in southern states added colorful detail to descriptions of Chicago as a promised land.[2] Such tales of opportunities were legion: better jobs, better salaries, better education, more dignified treatment from whites. Many black southerners perceived Chicago as an oasis of opportunity. These stories were told in churches, in barbershops and beauty salons, and in other public spaces.[3] In their letters home to family and friends, black southern migrants living in Chicago added intrigue to already-fabled narratives about the city's many professional and recreational opportunities and events. One migrant wrote to a friend back home, "I wish you could have been here to see those games. . . . Please tell J—— that he will never see nothing as long as he stay down there behind the sun. There something to see up here all the time."[4] In his youth, bluesman Tampa Red recalled Pullman porters evoking Chicago as "God's Country."[5] While many eventually found these visions and expectations exaggerated, testimonies about the city's opportunities were compelling enough to prompt a massive exodus northward.

The city's prime location inspired many African Americans southerners to view it in almost divine terms. Chicago was a transportation hub between the largely industrial East Coast and the Great Plains, and it served as a prime destination for European immigrants and African Americans attempting to find work in a growing industrial economy dependent upon steel mills, stockyards, and packinghouses. At the start of World War I, when the demand for unskilled workers increased to fuel the wartime factory output in Chicago, waves of African American southerners migrated to the city in search of opportunity.[6] Similarly, the start of World War II created opportunities for many African Americans in Chicago. Thousands found work in electrical and light-manufacturing industries. Increasing numbers of blacks found managerial and clerical positions. In 1941, the Illinois state legislature passed legislation that made it a misdemeanor for wartime industry to refuse to hire applicants "on the basis of race, color, or creed." However, as of May 1945, there had been no convictions under this bill.[7]

Unlike many of his black southern kin pursuing work in Chicago's wartime economy, Evans wasn't interested in a career in factory labor. He planned to start a career as a mortician. "I wanted to be successful, and the only black person who was successful in town was an undertaker," Evans said, referring to Charles Allen Rawls, then owner of the Rawls Funeral Home in Brownsville. "So I came to Chicago to be a mortician." It made sense to follow in similar footsteps. Such a profession would surely be profitable enough to snag Evans and his family from the tight grip of poverty.[8] Evans dropped out of Carver High School in 1945 at the age of twenty-one to carry out plans to move to Chicago. "I asked my mother if could I leave home. She had this relative in Saint Louis. . . . But I said I'd rather go to Chicago than Saint Louis."

Timuel Black describes how the decision to move north during the 1940s changed life drastically for many African American southerners like Evans. "The major differences would be that he now could feel a sense of security from the rather barbaric conditions that he fled," Black said. "He would also have at that time a greater opportunity for employment that would almost more than double the income for the same hours and amount of work. He would also have the opportunity to participate and to vote and to elect a political person who would be looking out for him and his family, which would not have been true at that time in Tennessee."9

Both Henry and Estanauly knew there was no future for their son in Brownsville. They had friends, Bill and Sugar Bonds, who had migrated to Chicago from Brownsville two years earlier in 1943. They made arrangements for their son to stay with the Bondses upon his arrival in Chicago. (Years later, Evans would move both his parents to Chicago. He recounted with pride that his parents lived out their final years far from the ugliness of Brownsville. "We brought them to Chicago, and they died in Chicago.")

When the day of his departure finally arrived, the twenty-one-year-old set off with his parents' blessing, no high school diploma, and no more than a few dollars in his pocket. That day he ventured to an unfamiliar land. Evans knew he'd be far away from family, but great anticipation overwhelmed him. Suddenly, the world seemed bigger. The bus ticket between his fingers was Evans's passport to a whole new world. When the Greyhound bus arrived, Evans boarded and walked to the back. Ironically, on his voyage to a land of greater opportunity, Evans had to ride as a second-class citizen. "You got a seat, but you had to get in the back of the bus," Evans recalled. He found a seat, and the bus driver pushed their foot to the pedal. The bus rumbled slowly down the road, then outside the city limits, and finally beyond Haywood County. As the bus picked up speed, the horizon outside the window changed dramatically. Green mountains turned into flat farmland. Dusty roads tuned into paved streets. Treetops turned into smokestacks. Farms turned into steel mills. Soon the lush southern countryside morphed into a concrete industrial urban metropolis. Time has now faded the many thoughts that swirled in Evans's mind during that bus ride, leaving only memories of his feeling of excitement.

Bill and Sugar Bonds, both born in Brownsville, had lived there as sharecroppers like the Evanses and carried similar psychological wounds. The Bonds left Brownsville for Chicago in 1943 for the same reasons Evans left in 1945. Clay Evans's oldest brother, Alonzo, had been married to a woman named Cloak, who was Bill Bonds's sister. Though Alonzo and Cloak had divorced by the time Clay Evans moved to Chicago, the two families remained close. The Bondses were pleased to open their Chicago home to Evans. This network of extended family awaiting the reception of blood relatives and friends from the South was a celebrated tradition among black communities in Chicago at the time. Those southerners who were already established in Chicago served as lifelines for those who came after them, seeking asylum and new lives outside the South.

After a day's journey, Evans's bus finally pulled into Chicago and headed downtown. Upon reaching the bus station on 12th Street, Evans was struck by the many symbols of America's grand democratic ideals and promises literally decorating the city's streets. By June 1945, World War II was almost at its close. The brave troops who had fought and risked their lives overseas were retuning to their hometowns. Throughout Chicago, locals were welcoming back their heroes with extravagant gestures of appreciation. Streets were crowded with uniformed men. Sidewalks were lined with flags and littered with confetti from parades that took place almost daily. Red, white, and blue ticker tape meandered along Lake Shore Drive, while various maritime vessels from rowboats to steamers colored the horizon with the Stars and Stripes. Everywhere, the city was celebrating America's victory. The air itself seemed to radiate excitement.[10] Evans breathed in the atmosphere. All around him were images proving that justice prevailed, that injustice didn't always win, that it was possible to overcome even the fiercest of evils if people possessed the courage to stand individually and collectively against it.

Bill and Sugar Bonds welcomed Evans warmly to their apartment on 31st and State Streets, right below the elevated-train track. In this particular section of town, known as the South Side or, more specifically, Bronzeville or the Black Belt, storefront businesses had been converted into apartments. Each storefront was usually divided into several apartments with shared kitchens and bathrooms. Sometimes two and three black families shared these common areas. Much of the city's African American population was forced to live on top of one another in these cramped, segregated housing units.[11] The Chicago Commission on Race Relations' report on the 1919 Chicago race riot offers a telling picture of the state of black housing in Chicago during the two decades before Evans's arrived in the city. According to the report, when black migrants were asked what they would change about their lives in Chicago, the answer given most frequently was the desire for better housing.[12]

African American Chicagoans faced poor housing well into the 1930s. By then, Chicago's Black Belt, located south of the Chicago Loop and stretching east to Cottage Grove Avenue, had become rife with segregated, overcrowded, and overpriced slums. At the time, it is estimated, over 230,000 African Americans lived in this area, which was about three miles long and only about a quarter of a mile wide.[13] Hoping to capitalize on the high demand for housing among black southern migrants arriving in the city, some landlords inflated rates for their illegally subdivided apartment kitchenettes, which soon became urban slums.[14] As a tenant living in one of these slum buildings testified, "Imagine having to spend that kind of money to live with roaches and rats."[15] Those African Americans fortunate enough to buy homes found their housing choices limited to the Black Belt because of discriminatory real estate practices and even intimidation, arson, and violence from middle-class white neighborhood associations that refused to welcome black families. A 1940 Chicago Housing Authority survey noted that about nine thousand black families still used outdoor bathroom facilities and about sixty-five thousand families shared bathrooms.[16] These horrific housing conditions only worsened when the United States entered World War II and waves of black southerners arrived in Chicago to fill employment openings within the wartime economy.[17] In 1945, when Evans arrived in Chicago, housing conditions for African Americans were notorious.

Like many African American Chicago residences in the mid-1940s, the home of Bill and Sugar Bonds was small. Still, Evans smiled when he remembers the Bondses' hospitality. "They made me feel at home," he acknowledged, gratefully. The Bondses' apartment had only two bedrooms and a hallway. Bill and Sugar occupied one room, and their three children—two boys under ten years old in 1945 and a teenage girl—occupied the other. That left the hallway for Evans's bedroom. He admitted his housing situation upon arriving in Chicago was less than ideal. "You were limited in your space. You were limited in what you could do. So you learn how to make yourself comfortable." It was a difficult situation. But Evans was grateful, he said, that the Bondses "shared their little storefront. That's all they had."

Although the Bondses were indeed gracious hosts, even their hospitality could not keep a particularly disgusting indignity from assaulting their new guest. The Bondses' apartment at 31st and State Streets was located in a part of the city where the sanitation was especially poor. "They didn't move trash like they do today," Evans said about the city's trash collection system at the time. People placed their trash out on the street, where it would sit sometimes for days. All the exposed garbage attracted rats. At night, these rodents crept into the nearby storefront apartments, looking for food and sometimes shelter from the weather. Because apartment hallways were usually empty at night, they were prime places for rats to lurk. They could conduct their business without human interference. However, since his bedroom was in the hallway of the Bondses' apartment, Evans slept in the direct path of prowling rats every single night. "I woke up at night, because I slept in the hallway, with rats running across my feet." The ritual was the same most nights. Evans would fall asleep in the hallway. Several hours later, the creepy sensation of tiny, bony feet scurrying across his skin jolted him awake. Evans dreaded going to bed at night. He knew that as soon as he closed his eyes, armies of rats conspiring in the streets would advance on his position.

Evans's experience with rats is strikingly similar to mid-twentieth-century literary and artistic depictions of African American Chicago South Siders' traumatic encounters with rats. For instance, in the opening scene of Richard Wright's novel *Native Son* (1940), Bigger Thomas fights a rat. The confrontation is so violent, so intense, and so chaotic that at one point, the incredibly large rat, frantic to escape, tears a hole in one of Bigger's pant legs with its sharp teeth. Eventually, Bigger crushes the rat to death with a frying pan. Wright's use of the imagery of this fictional rat is a powerful symbol for the real-life scenes of social alienation, racism, self-hatred, and economic hardship menacing many African American families living in the city's South Side slums before, during, and after World War II.[18] The fate of the rat in Wright's story seems to suggest that the larger social structures did not, would not, or could not protect the African American family structure from the pestilence of prejudice, poverty, and racial violence in mid-twentieth-century Chicago. Much like the rat Bigger Thomas kills in the opening scene of *Native Son*, many African Americans living in Cold War Chicago neighborhoods were cornered, terrorized, without options, and doomed to be crushed with fatal blows of collective prejudice, contempt, and systematic containment.

Wright's imagery of the ferocity of Chicago rats illuminates one significant way life in the urban North differed from life in the rural South. As bad as Evans's situation was—sleeping among rats!—he still preferred the four-legged rats in Chicago to the two-legged ones in Brownsville. "It was a very deplorable situation," Evans said about sleeping among rats in Chicago. "But I was glad to be away from Brownsville." He could tolerate diseased rats. He couldn't tolerate diseased racists. He believed Chicago held opportunities for him that did not exist in rural Tennessee in the 1940s. Wright, who made the journey to Chicago in 1927, would later recall a similar sentiment washing upon him as he walked out of the railroad station upon arriving in the city: "I was seized by doubt. Should I have come here? But going back was impossible. I had fled a known terror, and perhaps I could cope with this unknown terror that lay ahead."[19] In short, for Evans, as for Wright, the uncertain adventure in Chicago brought anxiety but also promised hope. Still, when Evans recalls those early days after moving to Chicago he admits he was surprised to have encountered such difficult circumstances so early in his journey. "If you look at me, you wouldn't think I've been through what I've been through."

Evans wasted no time initiating his plans to become an undertaker. Two days after arriving in Chicago, he made his way to the city's school of mortuary science. He informed a woman in the admissions office of his intent to become a mortician. Her response shocked him. The class would be for one year and would cost $800, which was to be paid in full in advance. Evans's excitement vanished. Frustration consumed him. Where would he get $800?! Chicago suddenly didn't quite feel like the land of opportunity Evans had dreamed about. His arrival in the city had not quite been the triumphant procession he had imagined. He seemed to face one bitter struggle after the next. On his long walk back to his rat-infested home, Evans prayed silently, asking God some difficult questions: "Why did you help me through high school and lead me all the way here to the city, away from my mama and daddy, my family and home, just to find out I still can't beat being poor? Why, Lord? What are you trying to tell me?"[20]

If Evans was going to become a mortician and rescue his family from poverty, he had to get busy making some money, and fast! But finding a job in the city proved a difficult prospect for many African Americans at the time. Even for those with a high school diploma, decent-paying jobs for African Americans in the mid-1940s were scarce. Though the North afforded greater occupational opportunities than the South, African Americans in Chicago were forced to mostly pursue positions in unskilled labor and the services sector.[21] "With no contacts, and with the influx of men returning from the war," Rose concludes correctly, "job hunting became a daily ritual of frustration and rejection."[22] For Evans, who had no high school diploma, finding a decent-paying job proved even more challenging. Still, when many did find work in Chicago, they saw their present situation better than the lives they had known in the South. For instance, one female migrant testified that earning a decent wage in a northern factory was a luxury she had not known in the South: "We get $1.50 a day and we pack so many sausages we don't have time to play, but it is a matter of a dollar with me and I feel that God made the path and I am walking therein."[23]

Fortunately, a few days after Evans had arrived in Chicago, Bill Bonds arranged for him to begin working with him, bottling pickles in a factory located at 49th and Racine. The factory had a conveyor belt, and there was a machine that jarred the pickles. "You just did whatever was necessary," Evans said about his first job at the pickle factory. The work was tedious. The job didn't pay much. But Evans was glad to be working. "We were taught to work, whatever work was." Evans was no stranger to hard labor. Compared with the sweltering fields and sunup-to-sundown workdays in Brownsville, working at the pickle factory was easy labor. Once he had a steady job, Evans began saving money for mortuary school. He breathed a little easier. But Chicago proved difficult on Evans's pockets. As soon as he saved a little money, there would be some unexpected expense. It was like he would take two steps forward and three back. Evans made the difficult decision to postpone his plans to attend mortuary school.

Evans lived in rat-infested conditions for about a year before the Bondses moved into a new apartment. At that time, he still had no idea when or if attending mortuary school would ever become a reality. However, Evans still had not lost hope that his circumstances would improve. None of the trouble he faced in Chicago those first twelve months—not his vermin bedfellows, his financial instability, or his deferred dreams—none of it could persuade Evans to move back to Brownsville. That chapter of his life was over. That much was certain. No looking back. Full speed ahead.

Still, Evans could never fully sever a feeling of obligation to his birthplace. And, interestingly, this obligation grew exponentially over time. "I did feel like, as I began to mature, that I owed something to Brownsville, just as the leaves of a tree that fall to the ground and soak up the moisture." He owed it to his family to make a stable life for himself in Chicago. He owed it to himself. He owed it to God, without whom Evans would not have made it as far as he had. So he tried his best not to focus on the negative challenges in front of him. Instead, he thought of all the blessings surrounding him. He had a place to live. He had a job. And he at least had a vision of the life he desired. So while Evans's plans hadn't quite worked out in Chicago, his mind was resolute. He would wake up every single day and face his struggles with the creativity, tenacity, and faith he had in abundance, thanks to his time in Brownsville. Now, lest his mother scold him, it was time to find a church home.

NOTES

1. Timuel Black, live studio interview by Melody Spann-Cooper, January 26, 2016, WVON Midway Broadcasting Corporation Studios, WVON 1690 AM, Chicago, sound recording.

2. Jennifer Searcy, "The Voice of the Negro: African American Radio, WVON, and the Struggle for Civil Rights in Chicago" (PhD diss., Loyola University, 2003), paper 688, p. 32, http://tinyurl.com/y7gpcxya.

3. James R. Grossman, *Land of Hope: Chicago, Black Southerners, and the Great Migration* (Chicago: University of Chicago Press, 1989), 92. For samples of notices in the *Chicago Defender* about southerners visiting relatives in Chicago, see columns in August 11, September 1, and November 24, 1917.

4. Emmett J. Scott, "More Letters of Negro Migrants, 1916–1918," *Journal of Negro History* 4, no. 4 (October 1919): 458.

5. Grossman, *Land of Hope*, 74.

6. Searcy, "Voice of the Negro," 31.

7. St. Clair Drake and Horace R. Cayton, *Black Metropolis: A Study of Negro Life in a Northern City* (New York: Harcourt, Brace and Company, 1945), 288, 292, 511.

8. Dorothy June Rose, *From Plough Handle to Pulpit: The Life Story of Rev. Clay Evans, a Man with a Mission* (Warminster, PA: Neibauer, 1981), 17.

9. Timuel Black, in-person interview by Patty Nolan-Fitzgerald, 2013, Chicago.

10. Rose, *From Plough Handle to Pulpit*, 16.

11. Searcy, "Voice of the Negro," 36.

12. Chicago Commission on Race Relations, *The Negro in Chicago* (Chicago: University of Chicago Press, 1922), 175.

13. Searcy, "Voice of the Negro," 36. Searcy obtained the 1930 population figure from Willie Dixon, *I Am the Blues* (New York: De Capo, 1989), 45.

14. Searcy, "Voice of the Negro," 173–74.

15. Betty Washington, "Negroes in Slums Charged 5 a Mo. for Filthiest Housing," *Chicago Defender* September 26, 1964, 1.

16. Ann Meis Knupfer, *The Chicago Black Renaissance and Women's Activism* (Champaign: University of Illinois Press, 2006), 3, 21–22.

17. John Collins, *The Story of Chess Records* (New York: Bloomsbury, 1998), 14–15.

18. For further reading on US policies of black containment during the Cold War, see Nikhil Pal Singh, *Black Is a Country: Race and the Unfinished Struggle for Democracy* (Cambridge, MA: Harvard University Press, 2004). Also see Elaine Tyler May, *Homeward*

Bound: American Families in the Cold War Era (New York: Basic, 1999).

19. Richard Wright, *Black Boy* (New York: Viking, 1937), 228; Wright, *American Hunger* (New York: Harper & Row, 1977), 1–3. For more of Wright's thoughts on migration, see his work *12 Million Black Voices* (New York: Basic, 1941), 93, 98.

20. Rose, *From Plough Handle to Pulpit*, 17.

21. Searcy, "Voice of the Negro," 31.

22. Rose, *From Plough Handle to Pulpit*, 17–18.

23. Emmett J. Scott, "More Letters of Negro Migrants, 1916–1918," *Journal of Negro History* 4, no. 4 (October 1919): 457.

4

A HOME OVER IN
ZION

Somehow or another, music had got into my system.

—Rev. Clay Evans

BETWEEN 1946 AND 1950—Evans stood mesmerized in the middle of Martin and Morris Publishing House on 4312 South Indiana Avenue. The studio, which had opened its doors in 1940, housed stacks of sheet music by some of America's most talented gospel artists. These artists' songs had ignited spiritual fervor within African American churches across the country. Evans combed excitedly through the stacks of musical masterpieces. By this time, Martin and Morris Music Studio had gained prominence as the country's leading publisher of black gospel music. It was a primary resource for any local pastor, church leader, musician, or up-and-coming singer interested in upgrading his or her congregation's music ministry. It was also a popular destination for many up-and-coming songwriters seeking to have their songs published. In the 1940s, it was the foremost black publishing house of African American gospel music. By the time the studio closed its doors in the late 1980s, it was the nation's oldest continuously running black gospel music publishing company.[1]

Martin and Morris Publishing House was the creation of Sallie Martin (1896–1988) and Kenneth Morris (1917–1988). The two first met at the historic First Church of Deliverance in Chicago, where Rev. Clarence H. Cobbs was senior pastor. Morris was the church's organist, and Martin directed the choir. The publishing house soon acquired the largest archive of black musicians around. Some of the more prominent musicians whose works Martin and Morris published include William H. Brewster, Dorothy Love Coates, Lucie Campbell, Alex Bradford, Sam Cooke, and Raymond Rasberry.[2] By the mid-1950s, the studio generated about $200,000 annually in revenues and royalties.[3] There was no question, Evans said, back then that Martin and Morris was the country's premier publishing house for black gospel music. "All the gospel music in the forties—they handled it."

By that day when Evans scoured through thousands of pages of sheet music at Martin and Morris, the publishing house had become a household name in black communities like Brownsville. When Evans's mother worked as the music director of Woodlawn Baptist Church, she sometimes ordered music from Martin and Morris. The publishing firm was a vibrant mecca where weary travelers could nourish themselves in the soothing currents of the black soul music that had nourished their ancestors since slavery. For black people, that music, that black soul music, said Dorothy June Rose, was "an unbroken thread running throughout history. . . . A thread that might twist but never tear under master's whip or ghetto prison."[4] Forged in the fiery furnace of racial terror, black soul music had had a profound impact on Evans before he even arrived in Chicago. From his earliest memories, this music was always buzzing in the background, whether in church or at home. "Some of his earliest memories were of his mother, humming as she went about her work or singing quietly to calm a fretful baby," Rose said.

However, Evans visited Martin and Morris Publishing House not simply to bask in the fame of the publishing house. He had actually begun to discern within himself an unrelenting passion for singing. "Somehow or another, music had got into my system." While browsing through the sheet music at Martin and Morris, Evans noticed another gentleman a few feet away. The man was Reverend Barker (Evans could not recall his first name). Reverend Barker served as director of the youth choir at Tabernacle Missionary Baptist Church, where Rev. Louis Rawls was senior pastor. Like Evans, Reverend Barker had come to Martin and Morris that day looking for new music. "Things just happen," Evans said, explaining the chance encounter with Reverend Barker. The two began a casual conversation. Evans told Barker about his interest in singing. Barker was so impressed with Evans's energy and passion for music that he invited him to attend church that Sunday at Tabernacle

Missionary Baptist Church. For Evans, the invitation was not strange. It was familiar, even expected. Growing up in a house with a mother so devoted to church, Evans thought of church attendance as the most basic obligation for a person of faith. As a new transplant in Chicago, Evans was in search of a church home. "That's one of the first things you were supposed to do," Evans explained about a family's expectation for their loved one to find a church as soon as possible after moving to a new city. Evans accepted Reverend Barker's invitation to worship at Tabernacle that Sunday.

That Sunday morning, Evans walked through the doors of Tabernacle Missionary Baptist Church on 4230 South Indiana Avenue for the 11:00 a.m. service. The building was an elegant edifice. "It was an attractive building," Evans recalled. "Everything was up to date." The congregation was growing steadily. "Back then, it was one of the leading churches," Evans remembered. Like Evans, many of the church members at Tabernacle had southern roots. Church members welcomed Evans warmly. After the service, Reverend Barker introduced Evans to some church leaders, including the church's pastor, Rev. Louis Rawls.[5] "It was going up at that time, not going down," Evans said about the church's growth. "Somehow or another, it just appealed to me to worship there. So I did." A month after Evans's first visit to Tabernacle, he decided to become an official member of the church.

After making Tabernacle his church home, Evans felt an overwhelming urge to participate in one ministry in particular—the music ministry. Evans couldn't read music. He couldn't play any instruments. But he discovered he had a unique singing voice. He had never sung much outside of church, growing up. But he found the power black soul music artists wielded mesmerizing. He envisioned himself one day singing on stage just like the crooners who had dazzled him as a child each evening on the family radio in Brownsville. At some point—it's impossible to say when for certain—Evans discovered he too had the power of a crooner. He learned he too could convert the invisible melodies swirling in his head effortlessly into marvelous hums, moans, and singing. Incredibly, without any formal training and without much practice, Evans's voice had become a powerful instrument.

Music had enveloped Evans's entire childhood. He heard singing at Woodlawn Baptist Church. He heard singing in fields as he and his family labored under the hot sun. He never had a formal singing coach. His coach was the church, his home, and the sharecropping fields. Over time, these environments tuned Evans's ears and voice such that he could produce a raw yet relatable and soulful sound. However, Evans did not actually begin singing individually in public until he moved to Chicago. "I never heard him sing much," his sister Lou Della said, thinking over their childhood. In fact, Lou Della never recalled having heard her brother sing individually in public until after he became the founding pastor of Fellowship Missionary Baptist Church in 1950. "The most singing I heard was after we organized [Fellowship]." By the time Evans endeavored to join Tabernacle's music ministry, his voice had been forged in the soulful, folksy melodies of southern black secular and religious musical traditions. Evans intuitively absorbed the cadences and styles and tones and pitches of singing ancestors and elders whose reverent chords emanated resiliently from the anguish of southern slavery and sharecropping. In short, Evans's stalwart ancestors graciously bequeathed to him a variety of gifts—the creative nuancing of standard musical notes, ears attuned to perfect pitch, and precise breathing techniques.

Evans decided to join Tabernacle's young-adult choir and sang regularly. Occasionally, he'd be asked to sing solos. His voice appealed to church members, many of whom were also from the South and found Evans's voice a familiar one. Word of Evans's vocal prowess spread quickly. After working with Evans for a few weeks, Reverend Barker determined that Evans's gifts were strong enough for him to begin serving the church in a more official capacity. Reverend Barker recommended to Pastor Rawls that Evans be appointed director of the young-adult choir. It made sense. Evans was a young adult, well liked, and his musical talents obvious. Pastor Rawls agreed Evans was the best person for the job. Not even two months after Evans first attended Tabernacle, he was named the director of the church's young-adult choir.

Evans enjoyed directing the young-adult choir. The work was challenging, and Evans took it seriously. The choir rehearsed once a week for an hour. His new position was the most promising opportunity he had since he arrived in Chicago. After assuming leadership of the young-adult choir, Evans began receiving invitations for the choir to sing at churches throughout Chicago on Sunday mornings. Over the next two years under Evans's leadership, Tabernacle's young-adult choir gained a reputation as a strong, spirited, and good-sounding choir. Evans's high-energy presence attracted more young adults to the choir. He had found his niche. However, as the young-adult choir's director, Evans rarely had the chance to sing himself. He was eager for more opportunities to be on the stage singing. "It was in me to find an avenue where I could express myself," Evans said. After prayerful reflection, Evans decided it was time to launch a singing career. He had the talent. He just needed to find a platform that would enable him to sing more frequently. "The way to do that was for me to join a group," he explained.

As choir director, Evans came into contact with all sorts of singers, musicians, and managers. Aspiring, beginning, established, retired—he met them all. Along the way, Evans met a woman named Beatrix Lux. Lux was a local beautician who had carved out a niche finding and mentoring local singing talent. Several years earlier, in 1937, Lux had formed a quartet called the Lux Singers.[6] The quartet sang religious music at churches and during special occasions throughout the city. By the time Evans became a member of Tabernacle, the Lux Singers were a musical sensation in Chicago. After Evans had worked a few years as Tabernacle's youth-choir director, Lux approached him with an opportunity he could not refuse: to join the Lux Singers. As sometimes happened, a vocalist would leave Lux's quartet for one rea-son or another, and she had to find a replacement. Lux was familiar with Evans's talents as director of Tabernacle's young-adult choir, and a recent vacancy allowed Evans to claim a spot as the newest member of the well-known group. He accepted the invitation.

By the time Lux approached Evans, Bertha Melson and James Cleveland were members of the Lux Singers. Cleve-land was a teenager at the time. "He was just a kid," Evans recalled. "But he could play, and he had showmanship." The energy of the group was dynamic. This particular ensemble of the Lux Singers gained their own following throughout Chicago. As a member of the group, Evans began to gain more popularity. And at Tabernacle, as a member of the Lux Singers, Evans's defining characteristic as a church leader became singing. "It was great!" Evans exclaims. "I came into a singing career. And to join up with a group like *that?!*"

As one of the Lux Singers, Evans met a host of aspiring artists who would, like Cleveland, go on to become famous singers. For instance, while he was with the Lux Singers, Evans met a young man named Sam Cooke. When the two met, Cooke was singing with another group. "Sam was with the Soul Stirrers. I was with the Lux Singers." The two would go on to forge a close friendship. However, Evans laments, "He and I never recorded anything together." Cooke would eventually become a member of Evans's future church, Fellowship Missionary Baptist Church, in the mid-1950s. About a decade later, Evans would preach at Cooke's Chicago funeral service at Tabernacle after the singer was fatally shot on December 11, 1964. In a February 1965 issue of *Ebony* magazine, writer Louie Robinson's article entitled "The Tragic Death of Sam Cooke: Shooting of Singer Shocks Followers" included a photo caption that described mourners "jammed" in Tabernacle for Cooke's funeral service. About two thousand people crammed inside the church for the 8:00 p.m. funeral service, and about as many were reported standing outside the church with temperatures at or below zero.[7] Although Evans doesn't remember the content of the sermon he delivered at Cooke's funeral, both the *Ebony* article and Peter Guralnick in *Dream Boogie: The Triumph of Sam Cooke* quote Evans as saying to the crowd of mourners, "We must strive in the midst of our grief to build a world where men will not need to perish in the prime of their lives with their mature songs still unsung."[8]

Evans found his career with the Lux Singers very rewarding. The quartet finally provided him a large enough platform from which to express his passion for singing. "Once I got with the Lux Singers, that kind of fulfilled my anxiety. . . . That just kind of took care of my hunger, my craving." Evans sang with the Lux Singers for about four years.

But although he enjoyed singing in churches across the city, he could not shake his desire to sing on the secular stage. Ever since those nights in Brownsville he had spent with his ear to the radio, listening to the big bands of Memphis and other southern cities, he imagined himself singing in front of large audiences on a secular stage. He couldn't ignore the burning any longer. He made up his mind. He

71

would pursue a career as a secular singer. Two years earlier, a friend had found Evans a job as a porter at the Brass Rail, a well-known downtown bar then located on West Randolph.[9] During the day, Evans would drag up cases of alcohol from the basement and restock the bar before evening customers arrived. The pay was a little better than the pickle factory, and the work was less monotonous. However, the Brass Rail appealed to Evans in a more important way. In the 1940s, the bar was located directly above a prominent cocktail lounge called the Band Box.[10] The Band Box, which opened in the evenings and welcomed many big musical acts, had acquired a reputation throughout Chicago as a first-class venue for entertainment, dancing, and singing. Thus, it was an ideal environment for an aspiring singer. Many flocked there on the weekends to hear performances from musical greats such as Cab Calloway and Lionel Hampton.

The Band Box was not the only nightclub on the block. During the 1940s, Randolph Street had become a major thoroughfare for jazz and blues music in Chicago. Next door to the Band Box was the Garrick Theater Lounge. The street-level portion of the lounge was called Garrick Bar, and the downstairs venue was called the Downbeat Room. Randolph Street was the place to hear the dynamic, sax-driven, jump blues and rhythm-and-blues bands popular during the 1940s and early '50s.

Working as a porter at the Brass Rail was the perfect gig for Evans. It paid the twenty-three-year-old's bills. It provided the right environment for him to get his big break.

The job enabled him to be in proximity to the big-band singers he listened to on the radio during his childhood. Since childhood, he dreamed of singing on stage with these musicians. Looking back, Evans said, "I think it was just in my genes as it relates to music. . . . I was trying to find an avenue to express it, give voice to it. . . . I wanted to be big." Evans explained his dream of singing on a stage with a big band, despite his early shyness and lack of self-confidence, as the expression of a passion for singing that was placed inside of him—given from someplace beyond him, almost as if it was his duty, his responsibility, his calling to sing.

Most of the musicians who played at the Band Box arrived earlier in the day to rehearse. Evans often witnessed these singers in the midst of their creative process. He peeked around corners. He walked a little slower. He intentionally took his time with his duties, so that he could study these black musical greats in their element. Evans got an informal musical education daily in that unconventional urban conservatory. Those once-disembodied voices filtering and flittering amorphously through his family radio now took on magnificent flesh.

One Friday morning shortly before Evans's shift at the Brass Rail, a young bellhop stopped him with exciting news. Lionel Hampton would be performing there that weekend! Like many black musicians at the time, Hampton often held open auditions on the evenings of his performances to scout local talent to accompany his band as it toured America. Evans was determined to take advantage of the opportunity. Expecting these musicians to rehearse for their evening performance in the afternoon, Evans would approach Hampton while he rehearsed. It was a common strategy among many African Americans hoping to launch music careers in Chicago in the 1940s. In fact, scholar Adam Green says, many "aspiring talents held entry-level jobs at the clubs, waiting for important breaks." For example, in 1943, Dinah Washington, who was working as a bathroom attendant in a nightclub washroom, signed her first singing contract with Lionel Hampton's band after "an impromptu performance."[11]

That weekend, Evans waited for the right moment. Hampton was casually poking away at piano keys with both index fingers, trying to harmonize the lyrics and notes of a song he would be singing that evening. It was the perfect moment. Evans made his move. He approached the musical giant. "Mr. Hampton," Evans said, interrupting Hampton's rehearsal. "When you get a chance, I'd like to know if you would listen to me." Hampton looked at the youthful Evans and told him to come back later that night to audition. Evans thanked Hampton for the opportunity and made his way to the locker room to change clothes before his shift. Evans's dream was within reach. He was thrilled. Nervous excitement surged through him. Finally, he would get his big break! After that night, he assured himself, things would be different. Things would be different for his family.

But while he was walking to the locker room to change his clothes, everything changed. It was sudden, unexpected, and forever. "The Lord changed my mind," Evans explained. He experienced an overwhelming feeling not to show up for his audition with Hampton. It was like a quiet voice speaking to him. Evans believed this voice to be the voice of God, who told Evans a career as a secular singer was not God's will for Clay Evans's life. Instead, Evans heard God calling him to pastor his own church. Evans was so certain he had heard God's voice that he believed—and still believes—that even if he had auditioned for Hampton's band, he would have failed. Evans said, "I believe that if [Hampton] heard me, I believe I would have had no voice." So Evans listened to God's voice and stood up Lionel Hampton.

When Evans's shift ended that night, he sat down at a table to reflect on everything that had happened. The weight of the moment was intense. He had heard the voice of God. He finally knew what he was supposed to do with his life. He knew what he was to become. He would indeed stand on a stage before large crowds, but not as a mortician or a secular singer. Instead, he would be a mouthpiece of God. As Rose explained, "His voice, his talent, his words, would be used to carry the Gospel message to people everywhere."[12] Retrospectively, Evans is grateful he did not audition for Hampton, believing now that he was too young and too naive to safely navigate the secular music industry. "I was not ready for it. I would have been dead, dead, dead a long time ago," Evans said, referring to the potentially dangerous temptations that often consumed many young singers. "I didn't know anything about that world. I came up in the church. Man, they would have messed me up. And I would have been dead."

Evans has no regrets about abandoning a career on the secular stage. That decision remains one of his life's most defining moments. It was the moment he walked faithfully into his calling, away from a secular stage and toward a sacred stage. "Thank God I went away and never went back," Evans said about his audition with Hampton. In time, the experience taught Evans that sometimes closed doors open wonderful new opportunities. "Thank God for closed doors. We only thank God for open doors, because we think that is a blessing. Some doors that you wanted open, if they had opened, they would have destroyed you. . . . I have learned how to thank God for locking some doors."

NOTES

1. Bernice Johnson Reagon, ed., *We'll Understand It Better By and By* (Washington, DC: Smithsonian Institution Press, 1992).

2. Martin and Morris Music Company Records, 1930–1985, no. 492, Archives Center, National Museum of American History, January 31, 2007, http://tinyurl.com/y99hffgm.

3. Wallace D. Best, *Passionately Human, No Less Divine: Religion and Culture in Black Chicago, 1915–1952* (Princeton: Princeton University Press, 2005), 189. Best gathered this information from Reagon, *We'll Understand It Better By and By*, 329–41.

4. Dorothy June Rose, *From Plough Handle to Pulpit: The Life Story of Rev. Clay Evans, a Man with a Mission* (Warminster, PA: Neibauer, 1981), 19.

5. Rawls founded Tabernacle Missionary Baptist Church in 1941. It is believed that at its height in the 1940s, Tabernacle had ten thousand members. He launched various businesses, including Brown-Rawls Funeral Home; Willa Rawls Manor, a 121-unit living center for senior citizens; a grocery store; a real estate and mortgage corporation; and a printing and publishing company. For biographical information on Rev. Louis Rawls, see Emily Biuso, "Rev. Louis Rawls, 97, Pastor Founded Church, Businesses," *Chicago Tribune*, May 2, 2002.

6. Robert M. Marovich, *A City Called Heaven: Chicago and the Birth of Gospel Music* (Urbana: University of Illinois Press, 2015), 161.

7. Peter Guralnick, *Dream Boogie: The Triumph of Sam Cooke* (New York: Little, Brown, 2005), 630, 632.

8. Louie Robinson, "The Tragic Death of Sam Cooke: Shooting of Singer Shocks Followers," *Ebony*, February 1965, 92, 96. Also see Guralnick, *Dream Boogie*, 633.

9. Charles A. Sengstock, *That Toddlin' Town: Chicago's White Dance Bands and Orchestras, 1900–1950,* (Champaign: University of Illinois Press, 2004), 173.

10. Colin Bratkovich, *Just Remember This* (Bloomington, IN: Xlibris, 2004), 83.

11. Adam Green, *Selling the Race: Culture, Community, and Black Chicago, 1940–1955* (Chicago: University of Chicago Press, 2007), 61.

12. Rose, *From Plough Handle to Pulpit*, 22.

5

A LOVE SUPREME

We didn't have our own place . . . but it has lasted.
That's the bottom line.

—Rev. Clay Evans

THE YEAR WAS 1946—Life as the director of the young-adult choir at Tabernacle Missionary Baptist Church was demanding. Not only was Evans responsible for determining what music the young adults sang each Sunday, but he also scheduled the choir's concerts at other churches and counseled choir members through personal problems. Evans strained himself physically and emotionally for the sake of the choir's success and choir members' well-being. During the week, Evans often spent time building rapport with choir members, listening to their troubles, and intervening in moments of personal crisis. All this he did while also fulfilling his duties at the Brass Rail. Strangely, at the end of each day, Evans felt more rejuvenated than depleted. "It was not draining," Evans recalled about his ministry as choir director. "Something that you enjoy gives you strength. The joy of the Lord is your strength. So when you start doing something that you like to do, it doesn't become a real problem. The joy makes whatever you attend to easy for you."

After fulfilling all his duties on Sunday mornings, Evans usually spent the entire day in church. He often attended Tabernacle's evening service on Sundays. But he did not limit himself to Tabernacle's worship. "Many Sunday evenings after the service, I would go to another church [to worship]," Evans said. "See, I was brought up in the church. That was my life." Similar to the long hours spent behind a plow in the fields of Brownsville, Tennessee, Evans usually found himself investing long hours, from sunrise to sunset, behind the gospel plough in the field of Christian ministry in Chicago. "Sometimes I got teased about that: 'Clay, what do you do for enjoyment?' That was my enjoyment. 'Clay, you just stay in the church all the time!'"

In addition to the joy of serving God, there was another reason Evans enjoyed directing the choir. Her name was Lutha Mae Hollinshed, born in Tupelo, Mississippi, in 1927. Her mother, Patty Hollinshed, reared Lutha Mae and her younger sister, Wilma Lois, alone following a separation from Lutha Mae's father when the girls were eight and four. Life then was difficult. As African Americans living in rural Mississippi in the 1930s, they experienced vicious racism, much like that of Brownsville. Patty Hollinshed endured one painful experience after another. She knew she had to help her two young daughters escape the brutality of southern racism, so she moved her family to Chicago. Like so many African Americans during the Great Migration, Patty and her two daughters climbed into a car and headed north. After arriving in Chicago, the family began attending Tabernacle Missionary Baptist Church. Lutha Mae and Wilma Lois became actively involved in the church, and both sang in the young-adult choir. Evans first noticed Lutha Mae when he began attending Tabernacle. She was elegant and proper, reserved yet confidant. She was an old-fashioned southern young lady. Her body language—every gesture, every smile, and every look—exuded her vibrant, easygoing personality. Evans still remembers the first time he saw Lutha Mae in church: "Pretty woman, *pretty* woman! . . . As far as I'm concerned, she was the most beautiful girl in the choir!"

When Evans first became a member of Tabernacle, he didn't interact much with Lutha Mae. He admired her from afar. However, after taking over leadership of the young-adult choir, he and Lutha Mae saw each other every week during choir rehearsals and on Sunday mornings during worship. "We began from that point communicating with each other. . . . I don't know the first words that I said to her. But we began a friendship." Not long after that friendship began, Evans started formally courting Lutha Mae. There was mutual interest from the beginning. Evans's daughter, Gail, recalled her mother telling her that she fell for Evans one Sunday morning after hearing him sing "I'll Search Heaven Looking for You." Gail said, "That's the song that she said got her." Evans recalled a similar story: "She was singing in the choir. I was waving my hands. She fell in love with my hands, and I fell in love with her looks." There is a family joke that Evans's talents as a singer are what appealed most to Lutha Mae. "She will tell you that it was my singing that appealed to her," Evans said, laughing. "Can you imagine that?! It should have been *me*."

A few months after Evans and Lutha Mae met, he asked her on a date. She accepted. "I was glad we got to that point," Evans said, recalling the excitement he felt when he realized his friendship with Lutha Mae was evolving into a romantic relationship. It was a simple date that took them to the hot spot of Chicago's South Side, the famous Savoy Ballroom on 47th Street and South Park. Baliban and Katz Management, white owners of the Savoy in Harlem, opened the Regal and Savoy Theaters in Chicago in 1928.[1] Jazz historian William Howland Kenny describes the theater as "the most elegant and expensive entertainment complex ever built in black Chicago."[2] When Ken Blewett, a black migrant from Kentucky, was named manager of the theater in 1939, the theater's reputation grew among the black community. The theater booked the best black talent and became a national tour stop.[3] During its heyday, the Savoy featured artists such as Louis Armstrong, Duke Ellington, Cab Calloway, and other great jazz bands. Although it mainly catered to black patrons, many whites came to the Savoy to hear and dance to the great jazz bands. The Savoy Ballroom served as a community center and a sports venue that hosted political forums, boxing matches, roller-skating parties, and semiprofessional basketball games featuring the Savoy Big Five, later known as the Harlem Globetrotters.

Evans and Lutha Mae spent the evening walking, getting to know each other, and dancing at the Savoy. Smiling, Evans said, "She was a much smoother dancer than I was. I never could dance, but I love dancing, love it!"

In 1946, about nine months after Evans and Lutha Mae began dating, he proposed. "I married her as quick as I could." The two agreed they would be married October 15, 1946. They couldn't afford a traditional wedding. Instead, they decided to get married at the city courthouse, which was near Evans's job at the Brass Rail. On the day of their wedding, Evans worked his shift at the Brass Rail and met Lutha Mae at the courthouse at 1:00 p.m. during his lunch break. "We got married, and I went on back to work," Evans said. "I was working that day. We didn't even go out to lunch. . . . There wasn't no wedding. No honeymoon. . . . It's marvelous when you can have a great big marvelous wedding. But that don't make it [marriage] work." Evans is grateful he chose to marry the right kind of woman instead of worrying about having an elaborate or traditional wedding. "We've been together sixty-six years," Evans said in 2012. "We didn't have a wedding. . . . I didn't have no money. My people were down south. So we just went to City Hall, got the license, and got married at City Hall."

For Evans, the most important thing was not the brevity of the wedding ceremony. The most important thing was "the longevity of the marriage." Evans was still living with Bill and Sugar Bonds when he proposed to Lutha Mae. The Bondses were living in an apartment on Indiana Street at the time. Lutha Mae lived on Indiana as well. Once Evans and Lutha Mae married, the couple moved into the home of one of the deacons at Tabernacle, who lived on 59th Street. Neither Evans nor Lutha Mae were troubled they did not have their own home. Staying with relatives or friends was a natural thing to do at the time. "When people came up from the South, they stayed with relatives," Evans explained. Evans and Lutha Mae were without their own home for about ten years. "We stayed with one of the members of the church first. We moved from house to house. We didn't have our own place . . . but it has lasted. That's the bottom line."

NOTES

1. Adam Green, *Selling the Race: Culture, Community, and Black Chicago, 1940–1955* (Chicago: University of Chicago Press, 2007), 58.

2. William Howland Kenny, *Chicago Jazz: A Cultural History, 1904–1930* (New York: Oxford University Press, 1993), 162. For more on the early years of the Regal and Savoy, consult Milt Hinton, interview (n.d.), tape 7, at the Institute for Jazz Studies, Rutgers University, Newark, NJ.

3. Green, *Selling the Race*, 59.

6

A CHARGE I HAVE
TO KEEP

Like good stewards of the manifold grace of God, serve
one another with whatever gift each of you has
received.

—1 Peter 4:10

The Lord had a stage for me, but it was not the world's
stage. . . . I was an instrument that the Lord wanted to
use.

—Rev. Clay Evans (2011)

SEPTEMBER 1950—Evans dangled seven stories above a
concrete sidewalk. His security belt was fastened securely
into hooks on the side of a window. The life of a window
washer was risky business. But Evans took great comfort
in knowing that his safety harness was designed especially
for window washing. He had left his job as a porter at the
Brass Rail four months earlier to work as a window washer

at North Pier Terminal on Wacker Drive. As a window washer, Evans had to come to terms with the potential perils he faced each day.

Evans worked from 9:00 a.m. to 4:00 p.m. five days a week, performing familiar rituals. He strapped into his harness. He secured the straps on hooks near the window. He stepped outside on the window ledge, then maneuvered around the exterior of the building. He applied the cleaning product. He wiped the windows until they were clean. Sometimes the job required Evans to work with a coworker on a steel platform that dangled alongside the building. The work was dangerous and monotonous. But Evans needed the money. It wasn't much more money than he made at the Brass Rail. However, every extra penny helped. Money was tight. Evans and Lutha Mae still could not afford their own place. When Evans took the window washer job, the couple was living with a church member. When asked if times were difficult financially Evans answered, "Oh, Lord, yes! You weren't making much money." Explaining their financial difficulties further, he said, "It was hard times. Somehow you live through those experiences, and you make it."

Evans was determined he and Lutha Mae would not live in the poverty each had known in the rural South. Some days, while dangling high in the sky and washing windows, Evans thought about Lutha Mae. He could not fail her. He would not. "A man wants to take care of his family. He wants to be a real man. So he does what he has to do. I thank God I didn't have to become involved in anything illegal." Lutha Mae offered Evans the stability, support, and devotion the young women in Brownsville had refused him throughout his teenage years. That kind of commitment, Evans said, is rare. "She was working when I didn't have a job or was in between jobs to support the family."

The life of a window washer was dangerous. Occasionally, the wind would blast sudden bursts of air, catching Evans completely off guard. But neither the wind nor the height intimidated him. "I was comfortable seven stories high." Remaining calm in the midst of chaotic and unpredictable environments was a virtue Evans had in abundance. It was a virtue cultivated undoubtedly in the fiery crucible of his days as a sharecropper in Brownsville. Yet this virtue would also prove to be one of Evans's greatest assets in his next and lifelong profession—pastoral ministry.

After his divine encounter at the Brass Rail several years earlier, Evans received clarity about the particular nature of his ministry. "Not long after I was called into the ministry, the Lord spoke to me about organizing a church." However, Evans is quick to point out that pastoring was never in his own plans for his life. He was adamant God had called him to pastoral ministry. As far as Evans was concerned, his call to organize and pastor a church was a duty, not an option. For Evans, pastoral ministry was an intentional, preordained assignment and not a whim. "That was not just something I *wanted* to do." Accepting the call to pastoral ministry, Evans explained, wasn't a minor decision inspired by ambition. It was a significant decision inspired by faith. "I was foolish enough. I had faith enough to believe God."

Evans was convinced he had heard God calling him to pastor a church. "It's hard to explain," Evans said about being called into ministry. "But it's an urging and unction. It's certainly not an audible call. But it's impressed upon your mind."

To be a responsible steward of the calling God had given him, Evans decided to receive formal training for pastoral ministry. He enrolled at Saint John Baptist Seminary (now known as Chicago Baptist Institute), then located on Chicago's South Side on 38th Street and Michigan Avenue. The seminary's president, Dr. William Johnson, became one of Evans's mentors. In seminary, Evans received the formal theological training he needed to succeed as a pastor. "I considered the calling to be in two phases," Evans explained. "One calling is to prepare yourself. So I started going to [seminary]." The other phase of the calling, Evans elaborated, involved the actual ministry assignment. "That had been my philosophy. Your first calling is to *prepare*."

While Evans was in seminary, many of his long-held religious convictions were challenged. New questions emerged. Unexpected interests surfaced. His skills for ministry were affirmed, tested, and strengthened. "It was marvelous," Evans said about his theological education. Interestingly, Evans's main goal was learning, not receiving a degree. "I did things differently," he explained. "I never worked for a degree." In fact, Evans would go on to attend one theological institution after another as an auditing student throughout his ministerial career. He audited classes at Northern Theological Seminary and then at the University of

Chicago Divinity School. "They would let you sit in class. . . . So I took advantage of two or three great schools that were doing that." While enrolled at Chicago Baptist Institute, Evans began seeking opportunities at Tabernacle that would help prepare him for ministry. "Eventually they let me teach Sunday school." After some more time, Reverend Rawls allowed Evans to preach his trial sermon. Evans can't recall the details of that first preaching experience. However, he believes he probably had butterflies. "I guess I was [nervous]," he said. He continued to take advantage of every opportunity at Tabernacle to learn more about the strange and wondrous calling of pastoral ministry to which he was now a chosen heir.

Having accepted God's call to begin a career in pastoral ministry Evans felt immense satisfaction. Although singing was in his bones, he began to discern that God had an enormous purpose and plan for his voice and his passion for music. "The Lord had a stage for me, but it was not the world's stage. . . . I was an instrument that the Lord wanted to use," Evans later expressed. Attending seminary equipped him with greater self-confidence. And though the twenty-five-year-old Evans still struggled with self-doubt, he believed God could help him succeed as a pastor. "I had a conviction that that was what the Lord wanted me to do."

Evans said he followed the Holy Spirit's lead and began making plans to organize his own church. He was diligent in his preparations. Over a period of three months, Evans sought out every veteran pastor he knew. He hoped these pastors would give him important advice about the journey ahead. He spent hours in conversations with pastors over lunch, on the phone, and in church offices. Evans knew he needed wise counsel, and he sought it relentlessly. However, many of the pastors Evans talked with were reluctant about his plans to organize a church. In fact, some urged him to rethink his decision entirely. "Some of them thought that I wasn't really called, that I wouldn't be a successful pastor." Others thought Evans did not have the administrative capacity to organize a new church. Still others thought he should wait until an appropriate vacancy opened. "They said to me, 'Clay, . . . there are a lot of churches, and some of these pastors are going to die, and you can be called to one of these churches that are already established.'" Evans resisted that advice fiercely. "I interpreted that as a vulture waiting for preachers to die, . . . but I didn't want to be sitting around like a vulture. I don't want someone to have to die [so I can be a pastor]." There were also pastors who were reluctant to support Evans's decision to organize a church because he was a singer who had no previous experience leading a congregation. "They thought that I wasn't understanding the struggle of organizing a church and getting it established. 'Why not just wait?'" But waiting was not an option for Evans. "There was a certain group out there that the Lord wanted me to touch, to reach. So I went toward them."

Despite dissident voices, Evans was certain about his call to pastoral ministry. He refused to let negativity influence him. "I felt that impulse. I felt that urge within, that that was what the Lord wanted me to do." The leading of the Holy

Spirit, he said, carried him forward while everyone else was telling him to shrink back. "I felt like I had to preach. Not everyone is called into the ministry in the same way. But you know that you know that you know. I felt that way about the ministry." However, Evans confessed that he frequently questioned if he would be successful. He had many limitations. He struggled with self-confidence. He didn't feel competent enough. He didn't feel outgoing enough. He didn't feel smart enough. The same thoughts that had tormented him in childhood mocked him in adulthood as he prepared for a career as a pastor. Doubts filled his head. How could a once mute, sickly, introverted high-school dropout be successful doing anything, especially establishing and pastoring a new church? "I didn't feel at any time like I had all the talent and ability to do it." In the end, it came down to conviction—an unwavering sense that starting a ministry was God's will for his life. "I felt like the Lord was with me. . . . I felt like the Lord had an audience for me. There is a group out there waiting for me to lead them. It gets into your spirit, and you can't get rid of it."

Evans held the church's first official meeting on Sunday September 10, 1950, at 3:30 p.m. at Winfred Harris Funeral Home on 49th and State Streets in Chicago. He invited a group of trusted family and friends to serve as the church's first leaders. Among those invited were his sister Lou Della and his brothers Pharis and Joseph. He also invited Bill Bonds's brother Robert and the members of the Soul Revivers, an a cappella male quartet Evans sang with at the time.[1] The list of those invited was small. But there was no denying the significance of the moment. Evans's calling, his vision, and his new life as a pastor were taking on flesh.

The morning of the meeting, Evans woke early. His mind raced between thoughts. When the time for the meeting finally came, people arrived promptly. Excitement buzzed throughout the room. Those gathered knew the gravity of the moment. They would have the important task of building the church's entire organizational infrastructure from the ground up. They would be the church's first members, financial investors, and administrators. All the labor necessary to launch and sustain a new church—drafting bylaws, establishing protocols, assisting with hospital visitations, administering Communion—all these duties and more would be their shared responsibilities.

Not everyone Evans invited to the meeting attended. In fact, other than Evans, only five people showed up. There was Evans, his sister and two brothers, and his friends Robert Bond and Arthur Spraggin. Evans was disappointed about the small turnout. He had expected to see the members from his singing group. Evans said he told them about God calling him to organize a church and that he wanted each of them to be a part of the new congregation. "They said, 'We're with you,'" Evans recalled. "But when the day came, none of them came to the meeting. . . . They had promised to be in the organization, but they didn't show up." Evans had mixed feelings about the lackluster attendance of the congregation's first meeting. "I was excited and joyful, because it was something that I wanted done." But he admits he had hoped for better attendance. "The guys who I had been singing with—they had promised to be in the organization, but they didn't show up." However, God had a ram in the bush. The five people who did show up had enough enthusiasm and excitement to accomplish all that needed to be done. Those five leaders rallied behind Evans during that historic first meeting. "So you have to get used to some of these disappointments as they come along," Evans later counseled. "They will help you to develop. . . . You'll never grow strong without some problems."

That first meeting was an important reminder for Evans that God does some of God's best, most creative work with very few resources. "Sometimes you have to step out on nothing. And if you step out, God will have something for you to step on." Evans's brother Pharis also recalled feeling many emotions during that first meeting, including excitement, pride, and anxiety. "Our first meeting of this church I was all of them," he said about the surge of emotions within him. "Afraid. I was excited, because I was very young, and I had not been exposed to anything like that . . . starting a church. So I was nervous. But it was a blessing."[2]

That first meeting lasted about thirty minutes. For the most part, the group discussed the logistics involved with operating the new church. Job titles were discussed. Responsibilities were assigned. Even a temporary location for the church was addressed. Evans had made special arrangements to hold the church's initial worship services at A. R. Leak Funeral Home, located at 4506 State Street. Then came the subject of the church's name. No one seemed enthusiastic about any of the names put forward. Then

Evans's sister Lou Della suggested the church be called Hickory Grove Missionary Baptist Church. The group all agreed.

Now that the administrative details of the new church had been addressed, one ceremonial rite of passage remained: Evans's ordination. His ordination was a necessary ritual to legitimize his ministry as the official pastor of Hickory Grove Missionary Baptist Church. The service took place on December 22, 1950. Other than the council of pastors who would facilitate his ordination, about fifteen witnesses, including friends and family, were present. The ordination council's primary task was to publicly catechize Evans. He recalled that the questions were fairly standard. "What do I believe about God, man, and sin? How do I understand the Bible? If the question wasn't simple, they got a simple answer," Evans joked. "There wasn't any kind of hierarchy, so they couldn't flunk me." After Evans's public examination, the ordination council facilitated a worship service in celebration and affirmation of Evans's calling as a senior pastor. Rev. K. D. Clay, pastor of Beacon Light Baptist Church, preached the sermon during that service. The excitement of that moment remains vivid in Evans's mind. "I'm eternally grateful to them," Evans said about the pastors who supported his ministry. It was the beginning of the rest of his life.

NOTES

1. Evans briefly sang with the Lux Singers, a piano-accompanied gospel group before joining the Soul Revivers, which was a male a cappella group. The Soul Revivers often shared local bills with groups including Sam Cooke's Highway QC's. See Horace Clarence Boyer, *African Americans and the Bible: Sacred Texts and Social Textures*, ed. Vincent L. Wimbush (Eugene, OR: Wipf & Stock, 2012), 472. See also Bill Carpenter, *Uncloudy Days: The Gospel Encyclopedia* (San Francisco: Backbeat, 2005), 135.

2. Rev. Pharis Evans, interview by the author, 2012, Fellowship Missionary Baptist Church, Chicago.

PART II

LAUNCHING THE SHIP

7

GOT A NEW NAME

Everything was a challenge. That's the reason why you have to be sure. You can't just start preaching because your mother said you could preach. It gets very rough. Everything is a challenge. You have to have that real, solid conviction that this is what the Lord wants you to do.

—Rev. Clay Evans

SEPTEMBER 1950—Around 11:30 a.m. on Sunday, September 17, 1950, Evans stood confidently behind the wooden podium in the small chapel at A. R. Leak Funeral Home at 4506 State Street. It was his first sermon as pastor of Hickory Grove Missionary Baptist Church. He looked out affectionately at the small group gathered. Fewer than ten people looked back at him. The low attendance didn't discourage him. "I had faith and believed that God would take that group and bless it, take that seed and multiply it." Evans was grateful he wasn't the only person there. "Anybody was better than nobody."

As Evans preached, a red curtain hung behind him, providing a colorful backdrop for the pulpit area. But the curtain served a more practical purpose: it concealed the caskets of the recently deceased whose funerals had not yet been officiated. A. R. Leak, owner of the funeral home, had agreed to let Evans use its chapel to hold Hickory Grove's worship services.[1] Leak knew Evans did not have much money, but he wanted to support the young pastor's new ministry. Leak agreed to enter into a special arrangement with Evans. Evans would pay Leak whatever he could afford in exchange for use of the funeral home's chapel. No strings attached.

Evans was one of several pastors to whom Leak had opened his funeral home for Sunday worship services. This kind of hospitality was a regular practice among funeral home directors in Chicago at the time. "Funeral homes used to gladly accommodate churches that were not fully established to use their chapels, because they weren't doing much business anyway," Evans said. "And if you could help them out a little bit, they helped you out by letting you use it. And you gave them something for letting you use it. So you helped each other. So that was a normal thing. They don't do that much now, I don't think."

Worshipping in the funeral home did present some challenges for Evans and his leaders. More often than not, when Evans arrived on Sunday morning for worship, there was an occupied casket in the pulpit area of the chapel. Evans recalled those Sunday-morning rituals he and other church leaders performed to prepare the space for worship services:

"When we gathered on Sunday morning, we had to put the casket in the back. So many times, I stood there preaching with a body behind me."

During the first two worship services at Hickory Grove, fewer than ten people attended. Given the small number of worshippers, the funeral home chapel was an ideal location for worship services. "We didn't need a large place with five or six people," Evans said. By the third Sunday, about twenty people showed up for worship. There was a lot of curiosity among new worshippers. They were interested in the young singing pastor with the raspy, bluesy voice. Visitors brought their friends and family members. By the fourth worship service, over forty people were attending Hickory Grove.

Because Hickory Grove did not have a large enough group of financial contributors, the church could not afford to pay Evans much of a salary. In fact, Evans's salary was twenty-five dollars a week. "I thought I could make it off of that. So I had faith enough to try. But I also had an agreement with the deacons and the other leaders that when the church starts to grow, 'Don't put any limits on me.' I had a good deal." When the church did eventually start to grow significantly, Evans explained further, his agreement with church leaders would enable him to determine his own salary from whatever funds remained after all the church's bills and financial obligations had been met, no questions asked. "That's the kind of arrangement we had. So I never suffered for anything." Evans had a specific philosophy regarding pastoral ministry and finances: feed your flock, don't fleece them! "All these young fellows coming in here now want to fleece, and they haven't fed them. You don't start at the top."

A small choir led the congregation in worship on Sundays, directed by Evans's sister Lou Della. Unfortunately, the choir director was not a paid position at that time. Lou Della was the only one of Evans's leaders with enough musical experience to lead the choir successfully. In Brownsville, she had taken music lessons and regularly played the piano during services at Woodlawn Baptist Church. A no-longer-published website about Lou Della's life and career said that during this time in Brownsville, she also formed and directed a group that sang for audiences in the area, as well as served as the accompanist for graduations at her high school.[2]

Given Lou Della's background in music, she was the logical choice to lead the choir. She tended it as a shepherd tends sheep. Lou Della later recalled the commitment of the faithful few who sang in the choir at the beginning: "The choir started out probably with about four members," she said. "We were six people in the organizing of the church. And Reverend [Clay Evans] wasn't a part of the choir, and my other brother couldn't sing, so he wasn't a part of the choir."

The tenor of Hickory Grove's worship services was more introspective and less visibly energetic. Evans didn't like this worship atmosphere at all. He was determined to slowly integrate more charismatic, emotive styles of worship into his church. "I was a Baptist," he later explained. "But people always said I was more like Church of God in Christ."

The first few months of Hickory Grove's life were challenging. Evans and his leaders found that sustaining a new church plant was exhausting, often frustrating labor. When asked whether the first few months of Hickory Grove's life were a time of victories, accomplishments, and development, Evans responded quickly, "There were none." Yet he felt a sense of fulfillment even amid the challenges. "All of them were tough days but joyous days." Evans found comfort in his unflinching belief that God had called him to start the church. "You feel you're on the right road, and even though you can't see a light at the end of the tunnel, you keep on pushing. . . . But the determination has to be there." Determination, Evans often said, determines one's destination. "Every stage in life carries along with it its problems. The older you get in life, you begin to look back and think about Romans 8:28, that all things work together for the good." Evans came to view challenges, problems, and unexpected hurdles as sacred moments during which people of faith can bring people closer to God. "I've always had problems. . . . There are challenges. But you know that they work together like a jigsaw puzzle; when they're all put together, you'll see a full picture. The Lord is putting it together for our lives," Evans resolved. Adversities, he declared, can become powerful stimuli that propel people to higher heights. "All of those [challenges] that I ran into were just a boost. . . . Sometimes your blessing is wrapped up in your problem."

Evans's certainty about his calling encouraged him to press forward during the difficult days that marked the beginning of his ministry as the pastor of Hickory Grove. "Everything was a challenge. That's the reason why you have to be sure. You can't just start preaching because your mother said you could preach. It gets very rough. Everything is a challenge. You have to have that real, solid conviction that this is what the Lord wants me to do." Evans continued, "You have to have a strong enough conviction about anything if you're going to stand. You will go through high water and hell, but the Lord will sustain you. . . . I have seen him sustain me through some trials and tribulations."

One of the most challenging situations Evans faced as the pastor of a new church was a lack of adequate worship space. By December, about seventy-five people were attending Hickory Grove regularly. Unfortunately, the seating capacity at the A. R. Leak Funeral Home chapel was about seventy-five. In just three months, the church's Sunday-morning attendance exceeded the funeral chapel's seating capacity. Evans and his leaders had to accept their new reality: it was time to move. Evans began searching for Hickory Grove's new location. His vision was to eventually build an actual church building that would be his congregation's permanent home. "I had a feeling and a vision. Without a vision, people perish. And then without people, the vision perishes. I've seen a lot of men die and their vision never became a reality . . . because the people, the members, wouldn't support it, and it dries up on the vine. So both of those are true." Evans knew it would be several years before the congregation could afford to build a permanent facility. Until then, he would secure temporary locations to accommodate his growing congregation.

While Evans searched for a new location for Hickory Grove, someone told him about a vacant community center located on 20 East 45th Street. Canaan Baptist Church owned the community center, known as Canaan Center. Church leaders had held services at Canaan Center before building a worship space on the same property. Since Canaan no longer needed its community center for its Sunday worship services, Evans saw an opportunity. The space was large enough. Evans chose Canaan Center as Hickory Grove's new home. "So I did them a favor, and they did me a favor. And that's what life is." In 1951, Evans moved Hickory Grove from A. R. Leak Funeral Home to Canaan Center.

About a month after moving to Canaan Center, Evans decided to change the congregation's name. He had actually never liked the name Hickory Grove. He felt the name did not suit a congregation in a major metropolitan area. Once the congregation had settled into its new home, Evans changed the church's name to Mount Carmel Missionary Baptist Church. Satisfied with the church's new name, Evans began the process to incorporate Mount Carmel formally as a nonprofit, tax-free organization within the state of Illinois. Several weeks after submitting Mount Carmel's application for tax-exempt status, Evans received notification by mail that the application had been rejected. The reason was that too many churches in the area already had the same name. Evans would have to change the church's name again.

Frustrated by this rejection, Evans sought out his mentor Dr. William Johnson at Chicago Baptist Institute, who had been one of Evans's professors. He scheduled an appointment for advice on how to proceed. "I went to him and explained the situation that the state wouldn't accept Mount Carmel," Evans recalled. Johnson went to his desk, pulled out a document listing names of Baptist churches across the country, and began reading the names out loud. "When he got to Fellowship, I said, 'That's it!' We've been Fellowship ever since," Evans said proudly. However, Evans added, "When Jesse Jackson joined, we called it 'The Ship,' because Jesse called it 'The Ship.' So we were known across the country as 'The Ship.'" The imagery was rich with possibilities, and none of them were lost on Evans. In fact, the image of the church as a ship became a powerful way to broadcast Evans's unique vision for Fellowship and the particular labor God had ordained for his people to accomplish in the city and world. Dorothy June Rose elaborates: "He saw a great ship, rolling across the sea of humanity, gathering all it touched into the warmth and saving strength of its strong, impenetrable sides. He saw a band of people, fellow travelers on the journey through life, joined together in love and caring—sharing, helping, reaching out to lead all they passed along the road to their one common, eternal destination."[3]

A year after moving into Canaan Center, the state of Illinois officially incorporated Fellowship Missionary Baptist

Church as a nonprofit, tax-exempt entity. The year was 1952, and the church's official name was permanently in place. Now the church could began its real work: being faithful to the mission the name Fellowship signified.

Looking back, Evans acknowledged the risk he took in organizing Fellowship. However, Evans remained convinced he had been chosen for a life of ministry. Pastoral ministry was God's will for his life. He believed that with all his heart. "That was my purpose; that was what the Lord wanted me to do. It seems like I put an awful lot on the Lord. But that's how I felt. That is my mission in the world. I felt like I could help people . . . and glorify God. . . . I gave my best to the church, and Fellowship gave their best to me." As he thought back to Fellowship's beginnings, Evans insisted that God had encouraged Jesus's disciples to take risks for the sake of experiencing a more abundant life: "The Lord carried them to places they would have never gone. The Lord carried them to heights they would have never seen. Man, if they had never left their nets they would have only been known in that area. Don't let no one confine you to just being known in a narrow place! Sometimes you've got to leave your *living* in order to have a life. . . . Some people are too busy making a living to make a life."4

NOTES

1. For biographical information on A. R. Leak, see Don Babwin, "Rev. A. R. Leak, Activist and Funeral Home Owner," *Chicago Tribune*, May 2, 1993.

2. This quote was taken from Lou Della Evans Reid's website, http://tinyurl.com/ya6s4sk7.

3. Dorothy June Rose, *From Plough Handle to Pulpit: The Life Story of Rev. Clay Evans, a Man with a Mission* (Warminster, PA: Neibauer, 1981), 39.

4. Rev. Clay Evans, interview by the author, 2011, Chicago.

8

IT'S GROWING!

I loved music. Most of the church service centered around music.

—Rev. Clay Evans

We wanted the best. It was a lot of hard work . . . but it paid off.

—Lou Della Evans-Reid

THE YEAR WAS 1951—When Evans moved Fellowship from A. R. Leak Funeral Home to Canaan Center, he had one primary goal: to transform the congregation's worship service. "My background was music, so I was always interested in music." Up to this point, the worship at Fellowship had been more reserved, quiet, and contemplative. However, Evans wanted worship services at Fellowship to be more energetic and participatory. He was determined to infuse the worship experience at Fellowship with a more vibrant, upbeat atmosphere. "I wanted my ministry to revolve around good singing, good music." It would be here at Canaan Center that a legendary music ministry would be born.

After moving the congregation to Canaan Center, Evans sang frequently during Sunday worship services. "I was doing a lot of singing," he recalled. His unique singing voice was attracting more people to worship services each Sunday. Evans had strained his vocal chords severely while he was a member of the Lux Singers. As a result, both his singing and speaking voice had developed a permanent gravely rasp. The condition gave Evans's voice a unique texture. Johari Jabir, assistant professor of African American Studies at the University of Illinois at Chicago, offers a compelling description of Evans's voice:

> It's very much about economy. He's a big presence. But the sound of his voice, it isn't a Dr. King kind of bravado. It's very much about the economy. A kind of penetrative economy. It's small in volume and even the sort of range of pitch. He's not very high, not very low. It's very small but it's very cutting. It goes really, really far. That's actually a really remarkable, peculiar thing about his sense of style is the economy of it. It's small but far reaching. It's very musical. And he has all the sort of southern affect. But it isn't about explosion in the way that King, you know, King has sort of a ring; it's large. But that's not Clay's voice. It's quiet, but it does this other labor. . . . The substance of it has a kind of economy.[1]

Evans's voice was unique. That much was undeniable. But the unique sound Evans achieved was anchored in something more than just musical prowess or strained vocal chords. Evans's voice was forged in the rural segregated South, where music occupied a central role in sacred and secular life.

Music was a critical part of the culture of Haywood County. Here the lines between "the church" and "the world" often blurred. In Haywood County, many African Americans experienced music not only at church but also at picnics, teas, talent nights, festivals, homecomings, and recreational or social events. Sharon Norris's portfolio on Haywood County in *Haywood County Tennessee* preserves these special moments with music.[2] In this part of the rural, segregated South the secular music of Saturday night often served just as significant a role in the life of oppressed African American southerners as the sacred music of Sunday morning. Both genres of music allowed black share-cropping families avenues through which they could artic-ulate their struggles and hopes for brighter horizons. For example, Evans described the blues and the spirituals being remarkably similar, since each allowed African Americans an avenue to express their ultimate concerns: "The blues were a close kin to spirituals. . . . The blues were related to the relationship between a man and a woman. The spiritu-als were related to the relationship between us and God." During Evans's childhood, the music at Woodlawn Baptist Church on Sunday morning was influenced by the spiritu-als and the blues, both of which black folk in Brownsville sang while working the fields as sharecroppers Monday through Saturday. Each Sunday as a youngster, Evans heard a mixture of traditional white Protestant hymns, gospel music, spirituals, and the blues. Over time, these genres, tunes, styles, and melodies saturated Evans's psyche: "I loved music."

When Evans finally began singing in public, his voice had been forged in the deep spirituality of southern black religious and secular culture. The black southern migrant in Chicago in particular could hear in Evans's voice the struggle of black life in America, the lament of bondage and the longing for freedom. Many black southerners in Chicago found Evans's voice so appealing because they heard in his voice their own story traveling along the stony road of injustice toward more hopeful horizons. People flocked to Fellowship on Sunday mornings because they experienced in Evans's voice a powerful testimony of lament and praise that they had known in southern churches and in southern fields, testimony they often failed to experience in the same way in northern worship experiences in the mid-twentieth century.

Several months after Evans moved Fellowship to Canaan Center, over one hundred people were attending Sunday worship services. The increased attendance brought enough financial resources to fund Evans's plan to overhaul Fellowship's music ministry. Higher attendance also meant there were more people who could serve in leadership positions. "We had to start to organize the infrastructure of the church," Evans said, referring to the significant work necessary to sustain the growing congregation at the time. Evans, along with his leadership team, created a variety of ministries, including an ushers' board, deacons' board, ministers' board, and several other auxiliaries. At this point, Fellowship had entered into an important new season. "It's growing! It's growing!" Evans said about the church's progress at Canaan Center. Seeds sown in the rockier soil of Fellowship's beginning had begun to bear fruit. "It got everyone feeling good. It got me feeling good as the pastor."

Evans focused most of his attention on building Fellowship's music ministry. He understood that for most of the black religious folk in Chicago, music was a vital part of their spiritual lives. "In the black church, there are three things that are most needed: good singing, good preaching, and praying," Evans said. Evans decided he would center Fellowship's entire ministry on music. His hope was that the right kind of music program would draw even more people to Fellowship on Sunday mornings. His vision was simple. He would model Fellowship's choir after the secular big bands performing at the time. The big bands of the 1940s and '50s were large operations. Usually, they consisted of a bandleader, several singers, and thirty or more musicians on stage at one time. "They were orchestras. They weren't just a band," Evans explained. These bands could generate spectacular energy in their audiences. Evans believed that if he could duplicate the big-band experience during Fellowship's Sunday services, then the ministry could attract large numbers of people to the church on Sundays and during the week. "I always believed in a mass choir."

Evans was not the first pastor in Chicago to style a congregation's music ministry after secular big bands. Several pastors had already been successful in such ventures. Rev. Clarence Cobbs, then pastor of First Church of Deliverance; Rev. Louis Boddie, then pastor of Greater Harvest Baptist Church; and Rev. Louis Rawls, then pastor of Tabernacle Baptist Church each had a choir with over one hundred choir members. These pastors' music ministries provided examples that inspired Evans as he sought to build his own mass choir at Fellowship.

To produce the big-band sound, Evans decided Fellowship's choir should have at least one hundred singers. Just a few months after Fellowship moved to Canaan Center, the choir had about forty members. At the time, Evans recalled, most church choirs in Chicago had fewer than fifty members. "I always believed in colossal, whatever that means. I wanted a big church. Then I wanted a big choir. And I wanted the church doing big things." Thus, Evans envisioned Fellowship's choir to be unique among Chicago churches, in both size and sound. "Coming from a musical background, naturally I would be interested in music, a good choir, a good musician. I had a taste for music."

To remodel Fellowship's music ministry, Evans would need the help of a seasoned professional. Fellowship could now afford to hire several full-time leaders. Thus, the first major step in building a new music ministry involved hiring a full-time musician. Previously, Fellowship had used congregational volunteers to lead the music ministry. Hiring a full-time musician would add a greater level of accountability and thus would lead to a higher-caliber music ministry. Evans would be a key part of the music ministry's new direction. His voice would serve as the choir's anchor. In other words, Fellowship's choir would be much like a big band but with Clay Evans as the lead singer! His sister Lou Della would continue serving as Fellowship's choir director.

Evans knew of a talented young Chicago musician named Willie Webb. Webb had made a name for himself playing at churches throughout the city. "Willie Webb at that time was noted to be one of the greatest organists that we had in the city," Evans said. Evans was determined to secure Webb as Fellowship's first full-time musician. About a year after moving into Canaan Center, Evans hired Webb as Fellowship's first music director. "He was a renowned musician in the fifties, especially in the playing of the Hammond organ," Evans recalled. The youthful Webb brought great dynamism to Fellowship's worship. "I hired him along with my sister [Lou Della], along with some other musicians."

For the first time, Fellowship had paid employees leading the church's music ministry. The entire atmosphere of worship changed almost immediately. Webb "was the musician of the city!" said Lou Della. "He was an excellent musician. People knew Willie." Rev. Dr. Isaac Whittmon, pastor of Greater Metropolitan Church of Christ, was twelve when he started attending Fellowship's services at Canaan Center. Whittmon recalled how Webb's ministry transformed worship services: "There was a great choir led by Willie Webb, who was a great musician. He allowed me in the choir, even though I was too young. But I could sing. I began to follow Rev. Evans's ministry from that time even to this day."

After Evans hired Webb, the energy of Fellowship's worship services shifted dramatically. The pace of worship increased. The tempo of the music became more upbeat. Perhaps the most immediate shift involved more outward emotional expressions from church members during worship. Crying, shouting, dancing—all these expressions were more openly expressed during Fellowship's worship after Webb's arrival. It was unmistakable. Webb's music ministry had helped ignite a fire at Fellowship! With Webb on staff, Evans could begin the difficult work of recruiting one hundred people to the choir. He could not afford to be picky. He couldn't recruit only people with formal music training. Evans welcomed anyone who had a desire to sing, regardless of their musical talent. "I wanted mass," Evans explained. "Even if you couldn't sing, if you *wanted* to sing, you were welcome. . . . That's why I had musicians; that's what I was paying them for." Throughout Fellowship's history, members of the music ministry included people like Albert A. Goodson, Charles Walker, Milton Brunson, Robert Anderson, Frederick Young, Willie Webb, Royal "Mickey" Warren, Stanley Keeble, Curtis Fondren, and Billy Jones.[3]

As Fellowship's choir director, Lou Della never held formal auditions for anyone interested in joining the choir. Usually, she would ask a person to sing a familiar song, such as "What a Friend We Have in Jesus." She later recalled, "I listened to where your voice was. I could pick up on it when I asked you to do a familiar song. I could tell about the quality of their voice." Once Lou Della understood the strengths and weaknesses of a singer, she knew how best to integrate that singer into the choir. And at every stage, Lou Della asked God for guidance as she directed the choir. "That's one thing I always asked the Lord," she said. "Lord, you direct me and I'll direct the choir."

Fellowship's choir soon became known as a choir that offered people on the South Side all the emotional effect of the rural southern worship experience found in places like Tennessee and Mississippi. The music was special. It was uplifting. And it was relevant to poor and working-class black southern migrants who had left their homes in the South in search of opportunities in Chicago. "It was something they could take back home and live off," Lou Della said. "It gave you something to live off during the week. And you were so anxious to get back the next Sunday."

However, the journey was not always easy. There were always a few naysayers, Evans said, who made his sister's job of directing the choir challenging. "There were some," he said, "who didn't want to work with her because they didn't feel she was qualified." But with Evans's support, Lou Della thrived as Fellowship's choir director.

It was at Canaan Center that Fellowship's choir started to grow significantly. "It started like a family thing," Lou Della recalled. "Family brought their families. We had a few people who came from Tabernacle [Missionary Baptist Church] who were over there with [Clay]." When Fellowship started broadcasting weekly services over the radio in 1952, it introduced even larger numbers of people from Chicago and surrounding areas to Evans's preaching and to the choir's dynamic singing. It was the beginning of something special. Everyone knew it. With this in mind, Lou Della demanded excellence from everyone who sang in the choir. Each week, she pushed the choir, at every moment, to achieve the highest possible quality of sound. She knew she had been given a special assignment, and she wanted to be faithful in God's eyes. "We wanted the best," she said. "It was a lot of hard work . . . but it paid off."

NOTES

1. Dr. Johari Jabir, interview by the author, 2013, Chicago.

2. Sharon Norris, *Haywood County Tennessee*, Black America Series (Charleston, SC: Arcadia, 2000).

3. Malaco Music Group, "Reverend Clay Evans," https://tinyurl.com/y8yun8yx.

9

REVEREND MOTHER YORK

I think when you do the will of God, he has a way of comforting you and strengthening you. You feel you're in the will of God.

—Rev. Clay Evans

Mother, Mother Brooks, the Lord has called me to preach, called me to preach![1]

—Rev. Consuella York (July 19, 1988)

BETWEEN 1951 AND 1954—An often-unheard part of Evans's story involves the friendships he made as a seminary student at Chicago Baptist Institute. He enjoyed every part of his seminary experience. The classes were challenging. The course content was interesting. The professors were compelling. Evans underwent significant intellectual growth as a student at Chicago Baptist Institute. He found the entire experience of formal theological education enriching. One aspect of that journey appealed to him more than any other: the collaboration, collegiality, and camaraderie among his fellow students.

Evans was surrounded daily by fellow black ministers—some aspiring, some just beginning, and some veterans. Like him, some were in their twenties. Others were much older. Evans found interactions with his fellow classmates invigorating. Conversations before and after classes about lectures, opinions about church doctrine, and abstract theological debates provided opportunities for lively and sometimes heated discussions between Evans and his classmates. These discussions were opportunities for Evans and his colleagues to think more critically about the subjects, questions, and convictions they would encounter as budding ministers and theologians. While at seminary, Evans had many conversation partners. But in terms of faithfulness, spirituality, and friendship, none compared to Consuella York.

Evans first met Consuella in 1947, when the two shared seminary classes. "At that time, it was certainly unique to find a woman in a seminary Bible-teaching class. I think she was pregnant at that time. She had a couple of kids and was expecting another." In the 1940s, it was rare to find many African American women in North American seminaries training to serve as ministers or pastors. Within African American Baptist churches at the time, it was not a regular practice to publicly endorse women in ministry. It certainly happened, but infrequently and often with little fanfare. This is where Evans was different from many of his male peers in seminary and ministry at the time. "It wasn't any problem for me to accept her," Evans said. As womanist scholars in religion have noted, since many African American churches then did not endorse women in ministry, black women like Consuella York unfortunately were sent to seminary with the expectation that they would strengthen their skills to eventually serve in subordinate roles.[2] "They weren't coming to be preachers, because pastors wouldn't let them preach," Evans explained. "They were coming to be more faithful leaders . . . to better their education in the Christian curriculum." Yet after meeting Consuella, Evans clearly saw that, despite widespread rejection of women ministers in black churches, she was a woman of faith whose gifts would not conform to church cultures that oppressed women in ministry.

Consuella was born July 26, 1923, at 4241 Evans Avenue on Chicago's South Side. Named after her mother, she was the youngest of four children. Her sister Elizabeth was the oldest, followed by her brother Gordon, and then her sister Ada. Her father, Rev. John L. Batchelor, was a Baptist preacher. Christianity was a foundational part of Consuella's childhood. In a 1988 interview, she recalled, "I was reared in a Christian home. Naturally, my father being a minister, church was a must. . . . So church has been a part of my entire life."[3] By the time Evans met Consuella, she had started a small business to generate income. She had a mimeograph shop at 3422 South State Street, where she typed the handwritten sermons of local black pastors so that they could preach from printed manuscripts on

Sunday mornings. Preachers would bring their sermon notes to Consuella on Thursday, Friday, and sometimes Saturday nights, and for a fee, she typed their sermons in time for Sunday morning.

Consuella's family attended Sweet Home Baptist Church, located just down the street from their home. Her father was an associate minister there. She recounts her early experience with preaching: "My father and mother would take us to church every Sunday, and whenever my father would preach he said, 'Whoever can stay awake and remember the sermon, I'll give 'em a nickel.' And . . . every Sunday evening, I'd have an orange crate, and I was going through . . . pantomimed my father's sermon, and never realizing what the Lord had in plan for me in years to come."[4]

As it turned out, Consuella testified, God planned for her to pursue a career in ministry as a preacher. She remembered vividly the day she received her call from God to preach. "I shan't forget the day the Lord called me to preach." It was the fourth Monday in 1952. Consuella was in her third year at St. John's Baptist Seminary (now Chicago Baptist Institute) acquiring education to be a better Sunday school teacher. "It was at high noon, and I was running my mimeograph machine, and very audibly, a voice . . . I heard a voice say, 'Preach My Gospel and give Me a clean life.' I mean audibly, not any muffled sound, nothing. I wasn't in a trance. I ran to the back of the place where my godmother was (her name was Mother Betsy Brooks). I said, 'Mother, Mother Brooks, the Lord has called me to preach, called me to preach!' And she was washing dishes. She just dropped the dishes. We were back there shouting . . . shouting and just having a time."[5] Shortly afterward, Consuella told her father she had been called to preach. But her father did not approve of women preachers. He told her not to say anything to anyone about her calling. "I guess that was just in his mind. You know, there are some traditional ideas that one has . . . and in those days it was a rarity for a woman to preach, 'cause he always thought of it in the masculine gender, about men doing it, you know. When you come from the old school, you know, you figure the woman's place is in the home, even though they are permitted to teach Sunday School, and do things like that."[6]

While Consuella was attending seminary, she was serving as the secretary of Saint John's Baptist Temple, where Reverend C. Milton Newton Sr. was pastor. Evans recalled that Consuella was received well by the faculty at Chicago Baptist Institute. "They were very proud of her," Evans said. "Consuella was quite involved. And they accepted her." Often, she would bring her small children with her to class. "She was a great mother, and also she was committed to the Lord to find out the will of God for her life," Evans said. "She was quite committed to be in seminary."

While Consuella was enrolled in seminary, she was involved in mission work throughout the city. She spent much of her time visiting hospitals and jails, ministering to the sick and imprisoned. She became especially known for her prison ministry. The Cook County Jail had a chaplain in the 1940s, but there were not many volunteers from the community who devoted their free time to hanging out with prisoners in the jail. By the 1950s, prison ministry in Chicago was still a developing enterprise. Not many lay church leaders, especially black women, were conducting regular ministerial work in Chicago prisons. Consuella, in contrast, visited Cook County Jail each week. She met with inmates, prayed for them, read them scripture, and preached to them. "They weren't doing it then," Evans said about ministers offering the consistent care and counsel Consuella offered Chicago inmates. "It was quite unique."

From the beginning of Consuella York's prison ministry in the 1950s, Cook County jail employees and inmates warmly welcomed her. The inmates affectionately referred to her as "Mother York" in affirmation of the tender presence she brought during each visit. Consuella's unwavering concern for the imprisoned, Evans said, melted even the most coldhearted inmate. "That's what made them fall in love with her. She would go into their cell and pray with them. She was very concerned. They all called her Mother York. This was our Mother Teresa. She took her ministry very personally," Evans said. White prison officials extended significant grace to Mother York each week. In fact, prison officials didn't ask to frisk her when she arrived at the prison. "They loved her and respected her," Evans explained. Evans elaborated further on the trust prison employees extended to Mother York: "The way these officials accepted her . . . she was allowed to go places other people couldn't go. . . . Even on death row, Consuella could go."

Jack Malone, who in 2013 was serving as a chaplain for

Cook County Jail, said the jail has changed significantly since the days Mother York was ministering there. In a phone interview on August 7, 2013, Malone shared personal experiences about his then-thirty-year tenure as a chaplain serving Cook County Jail. "We were more face-to-face, hand-to-hand with the officers and the inmates," Malone said about the prison's culture several decades ago. Malone spent time working alongside Mother York in the jail. At that time, he recalled, the rules governing visitors were less strict. For instance, during holidays like Thanksgiving and Christmas, the jail would cook holiday meals for the inmates, and Mother York would fellowship with them. "Times have changed," Malone said. "You can't have things like the dinners and stuff like that, because it's so crowded." Overcrowding forced prison officials to eliminate practices and traditions they felt might potentially compromise the safety of visitors or employees. "What they have done is they've cut all that stuff out," Malone said sadly.[7]

Evans's friendship with Mother York helped him recognize the need to strengthen his own abilities for mission work. He decided to begin shadowing her during visits to Cook County Jail and to the other places her missionary work carried her. "I was going with her. She was not going with me. Because I knew nothing about prison ministry, or the missions or hospitals, praying for people while they were there." These experiences with Mother York strengthened Evans's ability to minister beyond the walls of Fellowship. "I learned from her. I followed her lead. I didn't know what to do," he willingly admitted about missionary work in the early years of his pastoral ministry.

Evans learned from Mother York how to pray for prisoners, how to minister to those in hospital beds, and how to be a strong, pastoral presence amid chaos and suffering. "Her dedication always impressed me. Consuella was quite dedicated to doing that kind of thing. She had such a character about her." When it came to prison ministry in particular, Evans acknowledged, the most important lesson he learned from Mother York was simply to show up. "Number one, go! Try to give whatever comfort you could to help. Read the scripture and pray." It was common for some of Fellowship's members to accompany Evans during his prison visits with Mother York. Periodically during these visits, Evans would even see some of his own members behind bars. "Sometimes I got a chance to see one or two members. 'Rev, I'm so glad to see you!'"

Evans's exposure to Mother York's ministry dramatically shaped his understanding of how the Christian church should meet people's spiritual and social needs. "It made my ministry richer." This notion of the social role of religion served as the intellectual, spiritual, and theological foundation for Evans's own social activism and involvement in civil rights during the 1960s. Similarly, Malone, the Cook County prison chaplain, credits Mother York with helping prison officials and inmates better understand the role religion can play for those who are incarcerated. "We [ministers] do belong there. Religion belongs in the jail. I think it does help and I think that's what she did," Malone said about Mother York.[8] He had great admiration for Mother York during the time he spent working alongside her. "Humble. She was very humble," Malone remembered. At one point, Malone tried unsuccessfully to convince Cook County Jail officials to name a part of the jail after Mother York in honor of her ministry. "She put a lot of time in there . . . a lot of dedication," he said. It was no secret to anyone who knew Consuella York that her gifts for missionary work touched countless lives in Chicago. "She was very popular," Malone said. "Everybody knew her. . . . She wore a smile all the time."

By the time Evans moved Fellowship to Canaan Center in 1951, he had already witnessed Consuella's ministerial abilities for several years. He believed strongly in her call to pursue full-time pastoral ministry. But because of the prevailing beliefs among many black pastors in Chicago that rejected women in ministry, Evans knew Consuella's opportunities would be limited. He decided to use his position as pastor of Fellowship to support her ministry. Evans asked Consuella to serve as an assistant pastor at Fellowship. Accepting this invitation would mean she would have to leave Saint John's Baptist Temple, her home church for thirteen years. Consuella asked her pastor at Saint John's, Rev. Milton C. Newton, to write her a letter formally releasing her to work with Evans at Fellowship. Reverend Newton agreed and offered York his blessing.

Evans made quick plans to license and ordain Consuella at Fellowship. Such actions would betray the tradition that rejected women in ministry, held so sacred by many black

Baptist congregations in Chicago at the time. But Evans didn't care. "I didn't hesitate about that at all," he said about his decision. "The girl was all right. I had no problem with whatever she wanted to do." Evans licensed Consuella York at Canaan Center in 1953, just three years after organizing Fellowship and just a few months before Consuella was scheduled to graduate from seminary. The seminary had asked each graduating senior to list the title they held in their church, for inclusion in the seminary's yearbook. Now officially *Rev.* Consuella York, Consuella listed her title as assistant pastor at Fellowship Missionary Baptist Church. When the yearbook was published, officials at the seminary were not happy. "The black Baptists went into a frenzy," Evans recalled. The concern among seminary officials and local black pastors was that Consuella's title suggested the seminary was in the practice of sanctioning women in pastoral ministry.

Although licensing a woman for ministry in a black Baptist church in Chicago at the time was generally frowned upon, the polity of the Baptist church, which designates every local congregation as autonomous, allowed Evans the authority to license Consuella. "The sovereignty was in the congregation. We don't have bishops and popes and cardinals. And if this congregation and Clay Evans accept it, there's nothing you can do about it," Evans said emphatically. But Evans knew there would be consequences for licensing Consuella. "For you to go against our tradition, it was like violating the law. You didn't have to be in Chicago. The Baptist tradition just didn't recognize women preachers." Thus, fierce opposition among fellow Baptist ministers was inevitable.

News about Evans licensing Consuella York traveled quickly. Within a week of his issuing her ministerial license, talk of Evans's actions reached the ears of members of the Chicago Baptist Ministers Conference, a local coalition of black Baptist ministers in which Evans held membership. One of the members of this conference was Rev. J. H. Jackson, then president of the National Baptist Convention, the largest denominational coalition of black ministers in the United States at the time. Jackson openly rejected women in ministry. The Sunday morning after Evans licensed Mother York, the Baptist Ministers Conference deployed one of their own to Fellowship to confirm whether the rumors were true. "First of all, they sent one of the preachers from the Baptist Ministers Conference to see if it was so. So he came. I never will forget," Evans said, recalling that the gentleman sat on one of the front pews. Sure enough, there was Consuella York, serving Evans's congregation as an associate pastor. "He went back up to the conference meeting on Monday and reported it."

After learning that Evans had licensed York, members of the conference voted to kick Evans out. "So I was rejected. I'm sure that they were in touch with [Rev. J. H. Jackson], but he never talked to me." When York learned that Evans had been kicked out of the conference, she was deeply concerned. "She was very hurt about it, because we were close. So she prayed for me." It was the first significant public opposition Evans had faced as a pastor. In Mother York's

1988 interview, she recalled the fallout between Evans and some local black ministers after he had licensed her to preach: "They told Reverend Evans that, 'You will never be anything in the Baptist ministers conference because you had the nerve.'"9 Still, Evans defended his actions to anyone who opposed his decision to license Mother York. York said, "But they really branded Reverend Evans. Oh, that man took a spiritual beating for me, but he held to the courage of his conviction."10 Evans never doubted his decision to support his friend. "I felt very comfortable," he said about licensing Consuella. "I think when you do the will of God, he has a way of comforting you and strengthening you. You feel you're in the will of God."

Though the Chicago Baptist Ministers Conference rejected Evans, he had no intention of going quietly. The conference met each week on Monday morning. Though he had been banned from participating in the conference, Evans continued to show up to meetings. "I just never stopped going to the conference whenever I wanted to go and when it was convenient to go." Interestingly, members of the conference didn't try to stop him. Evans participated in the meetings he attended and was always heard on the particular issues being discussed, as if nothing had changed. "They never brought it up," Evans said about his attendance. "I was pretty powerful back in those days. They needed me. I didn't need them. They needed Clay Evans. And yet they needed to do, as a body, what they needed to do. . . . And now you find women in every church, ministering. Sometimes there are so many that you can't get to the pulpit if you need to," he added jokingly.

Eventually, Mother York also began attending meetings of the Chicago Baptist Ministers Conference. One of her professors, Dr. J. M. Royston, informed her that she was one of the primary topics of discussion at the meetings and encouraged her to attend and observe. "And so I went over to the conference and sat down, and when I looked in the front and saw who was fighting me, it was ministers [for whom] I had been writing their sermons for years," York said, referring to when she used to type ministers' sermons and print them with her mimeograph machine.

Though shocked at first, Mother York was not too disturbed by the lack of support for her calling to preach. In fact, she even found the entire situation ironic, given that the ministers' conference relied heavily on her for significant tasks. In addition to printing documents, sermons, church bulletins, and other documents for local black Baptist churches, Consuella York also edited the *Baptist Record*, the publication of the Baptist Ministers Conference. "I would do scripts for the *Baptist Record*, the Baptist paper, so they brought their paper to me to edit the information." Since Mother York was a topic of discussion at the time in the Chicago Baptist Ministers Conference, her name was mentioned frequently in the *Baptist Record* as the denomination's officials attempted to do damage control among the larger Baptist community in Chicago. And when York would edit the paper before publication, she often found it full of grammatical errors. Again, the irony amused her.

"And so I rewrote what they said. I said, 'If you're going to talk about me, put it in good English.'"[11]

Evans recalled attending meetings of the Chicago Baptist Ministers Conference with Consuella. Interestingly, she was received and heard. "They had to respect her. She was just a unique type of woman. She had it together. She went there for no other reason than Jesus," Evans said. York continued to serve at Fellowship as a licensed minister. But challenges remained. There were still people who would not accept a woman minister. Evans recalled that when he would be invited to preach at other churches, some pastors would turn a cold shoulder to Mother York. Some pastors wouldn't even let her sit in the pulpit area. During those moments, Evans stood by and defended Consuella. "My principle was higher than my politics. So if you can't accept her in the pulpit with me . . . reject her, you reject me."

On March 26, 1954, with the scandal of Consuella York's being licensed as a minister still active, Evans decided to ordain Mother York.[12] *Chicago Tribune* writer Paul Galloway later said in her obituary that York's ordination in the mid-1950s "was believed to be the first African-American woman to be ordained into the clergy in Chicago by her denomination."[13] Evans managed to find several pastors who affirmed Mother York's gifts for ministry and agreed to sign her ordination certificate. Evans was strategic in selecting Consuella's ordination committee. He did not select major power brokers in the Baptist denomination in Chicago. Instead, Evans said, he selected "little local fellas who were not in powerful positions within their denominations." Evans presided over Consuella's ordination service and preached her ordination sermon.

The members of Fellowship did not have much of an issue with Evans ordaining Consuella York, because he functioned as an autocratic founding pastor. "It made it easier. They didn't call me. I called them. Fellowship started out with five people. I used to rule with an iron rod almost." However, while that kind of pastoral leadership style worked well when advocating for a just cause, Evans acknowledged that such a style can become tyrannical. "You have to be very careful when you are in absolute control," he said. And while Evans was proud of his members for supporting Mother York, he was disappointed and hurt that there were some black pastors in Chicago who would not accept her. The attacks against Evans for affirming Mother York's ministry served as lessons that taught him the importance of loyalty and doing the right thing despite the persecution or hardship that followed. Ironically, not long after being kicked out of the Chicago Baptist Ministers Conference, Evans was elected president of the organization.

Mother York eventually left Fellowship to organize her own church, Christway Baptist Church. Evans supported her decision. "She had stuck with me and had done just a good job. Whatever Consuella York wanted to do, I was fine with it. She didn't leave to split up Fellowship or take any members from Fellowship. And I'm sure I told my members, 'Anybody who wants to go over there and help her, do it.'"

Looking back on the early days of his ministry as pastor of Fellowship, Evans acknowledged the significant role that

Rev. Mother Consuella York played in his own pastoral and spiritual formation. As friends and colleagues, both Evans and York shared a mutual respect, which some confused with a romantic relationship. "Consuella and I were very close. A lot of people thought there was something going on between us," he said, smiling but then stating emphatically that something was indeed happening between them, but it was not romantic: "It was respect!"

NOTES

1. Rev. Consuella York, interview by Robert Shuster, July 19, 1988, Archives of the Billy Graham Center, transcript at http://tinyurl.com/ydx3daez.

2. See Cheryl Townsend Gilkes, *If It Wasn't for the Women* (Maryknoll, NY: Orbis, 2000); Marcia Y. Riggs, *Plenty Good Room* (Eugene, OR: Wipf & Stock, 2008).

3. Consuella York, interview by Robert Shuster.

4. Consuella York, interview by Robert Shuster.

5. Consuella York, interview by Robert Shuster.

6. Consuella York, interview by Robert Shuster.

7. Jack Malone, phone interview by the author, August 7, 2013, Chicago.

8. Jack Malone, phone interview.

9. Consuella York, interview by Robert Shuster.

10. Consuella York, interview by Robert Shuster.

11. Consuella York, interview by Robert Shuster.

12. Fellowship Missionary Baptist Church website,
    http://fellowshipchicago.com/history/.

13. Paul Galloway, "Rev. Consuella York, 72: Jail Minister," *Chicago Tribune*, December 13, 1995, http://tinyurl.com/y7c6fzjq.

10

WHAT A FELLOWSHIP!

Somehow or another, that was the Lord's doing. As he said to Moses, "What's in your hand? A rod? Well, use it!" "What's in your hand, Clay? A voice. . . ." And it worked!

—Rev. Clay Evans

FALL 1952—Around 10:30 a.m. each Sunday morning, people searched anxiously for parking at Canaan Center. About this time each Sunday, the empty parking spaces would begin to disappear. Many rushed to the church before the 11:00 a.m. worship service in hopes of getting a good seat. Some of these worshippers lived in Chicago. Others traveled from as far north as Milwaukee, Wisconsin, and as far south as Gary, Indiana. All were eager to hear the singing preacher and his dynamic choir. This increased frenzy to worship at Fellowship started not long after Evans aired church services on Gary, Indiana, radio station

WWCA in October 1952. Many of the people who began flocking to Fellowship two years after the church was founded had been introduced to Evans's preaching and Fellowship's singing through the radio. "That's what people really came for, the music," Evans said. "I always did keep a good singing group." Thus, in the beginning, Evans admits, it was the music, not the theology or the preaching, that drew people to Fellowship on Sunday mornings. "We had a good choir, and I could croon a little. That's what most of my message was. It was the *sound*, not the message. We believed in whooping. That's what made a good preacher. A good voice," Evans explained.

After about a year at Canaan Center, the choir had about one hundred singers. Under the direction of Webb, the music ministry soared. Fellowship's hundred-voice choir was one of Chicago's most dynamic up-and-coming music ministries. Working- and middle-class African Americans as well as noted public figures were drawn regularly to Fellowship to witness the church's vibrant music ministry. As Fellowship's popularity increased, Evans decided it was time to expand the ministry's reach further. For Evans, broadcasting worship services over the radio was a natural next step in expanding Fellowship's ministry. In 1952, Evans began seeking ways to broadcast Fellowship's worship services over the radio. He had no practical experience in using the radio to broadcast a religious service. However, he had a vision. Evans believed if he could use radio to broadcast what took place at Fellowship on Sunday mornings into people's cars and homes, he could share God's good news in

Jesus Christ with more people. If he could reach more people through radio, Evans believed, he could draw more people to Fellowship each Sunday.

Evans had seen other pastors use radio effectively. He had first seen his elder Rev. Clarence Cobbs, then pastor of Chicago's First Church of Deliverance, use the technology to minister beyond the walls of the church. Music was a hallmark of Cobbs's ministry. Evans admired how Cobbs used the mass-choir sound at First Church to minister to people over the radio. Cobbs was among the first black pastors in Chicago to have a live radio broadcast of worship services. It was from Cobbs that Evans learned the benefits of using broadcast media as a form of evangelism. As Dorothy June Rose states, "His own deep love for music and his desire to be a truly powerful, influential leader for Christ, led Clay to adopt and emulate many of Cobbs' methods."[1]

Evans believed what was taking place on Sunday mornings at Fellowship deserved serious marketing. It was too special to not be experienced by as many people as possible. "If the commercial world can advertise their products . . . I've got a better product . . . Christ Jesus and salvation, and what the Lord does for people," Evans thought. He was confident Fellowship had all the right elements. "We got a choir, a good singing choir. And with my voice and a little doctrine." Evans only needed an opportunity to market Fellowship's best qualities on a larger scale. He recognized the power of radio as an instrument of ministry. Thus, Evans seemed to grasp intuitively what media scholars had concluded in the 1940s, that radio was a powerful public forum that could mobilize poor and working-class communities in urban areas like the South Side of Chicago.[2] Evans was determined to use radio as a tool to mobilize the masses through Christian evangelism.

Evans approached a local real estate agent who worked with local radio stations. Evans expressed his desire to broadcast Fellowship's services over the radio. The real estate agent then reached out to officials at WWCA in Gary. Eventually, Evans reached an agreement with WWCA that the station would broadcast worship services at Fellowship over the radio on Sundays at 4:00 p.m. The first radio broadcast of a worship service at Canaan Center, called *What a Fellowship Hour*, took place on October 19, 1952. The thirty-minute broadcast featured Fellowship's choir and Evans's preaching. The response was explosive! "It worked! People started coming from Gary, Indiana," Evans exclaimed. Letters poured in, asking for prayers, promising financial gifts, and expressing a desire to serve within Fellowship's ministries.[3] These requests almost exceeded Fellowship's capacity to respond. But Evans was excited to have that problem. All of a sudden, people throughout Chicago and beyond were talking about the raspy-voiced singing preacher in Chicago with the dynamite mass choir. Celebrities such as singer Sam Cooke began attending Fellowship's worship services at Canaan Center.

In terms of the format, *What a Fellowship Hour* involved one of Fellowship's members announcing particular moments of the service for listeners. This person introduced people reading scripture and offered commentary to help orient listeners. Later in the service, when it was time for Evans to preach, this person introduced Evans and his theme song, "It's No Secret What God Can Do." Six months after the start of the *What a Fellowship Hour* radio broadcast, Evans asked his dear friend Rev. Consuella York to serve as the person facilitating the commentary for listeners during the broadcast. Evans recalled, "I got a lot of criticism. She talked so fast that people couldn't understand her. But they got used to the way she announced." Consuella York exuded energy and charisma through the radio waves.[4] "There was so much spirit in her, in whatever she said, that it affected people. So she became a very significant part of my broadcast. Because the way she could present me or present the choir, it wasn't someone just making an announcement. It was what we call Spirit filled." Eventually the half-hour radio broadcast expanded to a full hour and aired from 9:00 p.m. to 10:00 p.m. on Sunday evenings.[5] *What a Fellowship Hour* would go on to air uninterrupted, though over several different radio stations, every Sunday for the next fifty years.

Evans was a firm believer in the power of broadcast media as a tool of evangelism. In fact, he was so convinced of the power of media to promote Christianity that in 1975 he organized the Broadcast Ministers Alliance of Chicago, a group of leading pastors who sponsored weekly radio and television broadcasts. As the founding president of the Broadcast Ministers Alliance, Evans used the organization to help ministers utilize their media ministries to facilitate various kinds of public advocacy. The group was socially active in the areas of health care and voter registration. It was an unprecedented means of connecting the media ministries of black pastors in Chicago during the late twentieth century.

To this day, Evans remains unapologetic about using media to advance Christianity. For Evans, the good news of the salvation God offered through Jesus Christ was the product Fellowship offered. "Advertise if you've got a product!" Though Evans had struggled in many areas throughout his life, he found his niche as a media master. "Radio was really my thing," he said. However, Evans has always been careful to acknowledge God for the success Fellowship's radio broadcast experienced. He even refers to the Bible to point out that God has always specialized in taking the small resources at someone's disposal and using them to achieve extraordinary feats. "Somehow or another, that was the Lord's doing. As He said to Moses, 'What's in your hand, Moses? A rod? Well, use it!' 'What's in your hand, Clay? A voice? Well, use that instead of using theology that you don't fully understand!' And it worked!"

Fellowship's choir had begun to find its rhythm. Each week, thousands of people in Chicago and surrounding areas heard Evans's preaching and the energy of the hundred-voice choir over the radio. Listeners heard the excitement during Fellowship's worship services. Rev. Dr. Charles B. Williams Jr., pastor of Unity Fellowship Missionary Baptist Church in Chicago, often listened to Fellowship's radio broadcast. Much as Evans emulated the Memphis preachers he had heard on his family's radio as a child, Williams listened to Evans during Fellowship's radio broadcasts and emulated him. "I would pantomime him preaching from the radio as a young man. I listened to his rich, baritone, melodic voice singing 'It's No Secret.' That song happened to be one of the songs, as a child, that I would learn and sing."[6] Those listening over the radio often came to Fellowship to hear Evans sing and preach as much as they came to hear the choir. "I had a product they could buy," Evans said. "The product was my voice, really. And they bought it. That was the amazing thing. They bought it—when I had absolutely nothing to say."

Evans's sister Lou Della remembered the large waves of visitors who began pouring through Fellowship's doors on Sunday mornings at Canaan Center. "Most people . . . heard us through the broadcast," she said. Indeed, radio proved to be an effective tool for attracting people to Fellowship. "People heard us who never heard us before. Our singing was pretty good," Lou Della said proudly. It was at Canaan Center that Fellowship's music ministry began to transform into a gospel music powerhouse. Much as first-century people came from surrounding cities to hear the locust-eating country preacher John the Baptist preaching in the wilderness, Clay Evans was drawing twentieth-century African American masses to Fellowship. "I considered myself like a John the Baptist, crying in the wilderness, and he emptied Jerusalem, Judea, as people came to see what he was crying about. So they came to see what I was crying about." But Evans was quick to emphasize the importance of Webb's role in attracting people to Fellowship in those early years at

Canaan Center: "Some came because of Willie Webb. Some came because of me. But they came, which was important."

More than his preaching, pastoral counseling, or administrative acumen, Evans concluded, Fellowship's choir broadcast over the radio was responsible for leading waves of people to Fellowship each week. However, looking back on the early success of Fellowship's music ministry at Canaan Center, Evans acknowledged that as important as music was in building the church's membership, music did not have the ability to build strong, mature, and socially conscious followers of Jesus Christ. "I loved music. And most of the church service was centered on music. That draws a crowd, but it doesn't really develop a strong church. Now my emphasis is different. I think you develop a strong church by preaching and teaching." Evans elaborated further, saying, "Music in the black Baptist church plays an important part. But in this new era we are serving now, I don't think they put as much emphasis on it as they used to. In the past, we didn't have as much of a message, so the music made up for it. We are learning more now how to teach, so we put more emphasis on teaching than preaching. Because we found out that preaching sometimes only works on the emotion, not the intellect."

Evans explained that whooping—a preaching technique in which the preacher uses his or her voice musically to appeal emotionally to people before, during, and after the sermon—was part of the tradition of preaching he inherited as a youngster growing up in rural Tennessee. Evans utilized whooping to attract people to Fellowship. However, Evans explained that as he matured as a preacher and pastor, he began relying less on whooping and tried to offer more intellectual depth in his messages. Evans told the story of the time he met a young man who was trying to whoop, and it irritated Evans. He approached the young man after the sermon and scolded him for being so preoccupied with trying to appeal to people's emotions that he had neglected to offer serious intellectual engagement. The young man responded defensively, "But Reverend Clay, you did it!" Evans answered calmly, "That was in that day. But this is a different era." Evans admonished the young preacher, "Stop worrying about *how* you sound. But worry about *what* you said."

Evans didn't mean to be condescending. He only meant to impart a helpful lesson he had learned to be true: words have tremendous power. Evans had come to understand how words intentionally used have the ability to mend what is broken, liberate what is bound, and heal what is suffering. Thus, Evans believed that those who preach to oppressed people owe their audiences more than zealous rhetoric. They owe these people strategically chosen words that can teach and inspire meaningful journeys toward more abundant life.

NOTES

1. Dorothy June Rose, *From Plough Handle to Pulpit: The Life Story of Rev. Clay Evans, a Man with a Mission* (Warminster, PA: Neibauer, 1981), 36.

2. See Paul Lazarsfeld, *Radio and the Printed Page* (New York: Duell, Sloan & Pearce, 1940); Daniel J. Czitrom, "The Rise of Empirical Media Study," in *Media and the American Mind: From Morse to McLuhan* (Chapel Hill: University of North Carolina Press, 1982), 130–31.

3. Rose, *From Plough Handle to Pulpit*, 40.

4. To hear Rev. Consuella York introducing Fellowship's radio broadcast, see "What a Fellowship Theme," track 1 from *What a Fellowship* (1960), YouTube, http://tinyurl.com/yc4c3nvz. She begins speaking twenty seconds into the recording.

5. Rose, *From Plough Handle to Pulpit*, 40.

6. Rev. Dr. Charles B. Williams Jr., written response solicited by author, 2012.

PART III

ON OPEN SEAS

11

LOOKING FOR A CITY CALLED HEAVEN

I believe the Lord will give you whatever you need to be a witness for him within your setting. Just use what you got. What you got, Moses, is a rod! What you got, David, is a slingshot! And I hold that true for a congregation. God put enough talent there to glorify him.

—Rev. Clay Evans

When you come into real leadership, you can only have one head, one real leader. But anything that has two or more heads making decisions, that's a freak. Anything with no head is a monster. There are some churches like that.

—Rev. Clay Evans

THE YEAR WAS 1954—Dirt clung to the walls. Cobwebs littered the rafters. Grease stains covered the floor. The smell of gasoline lingered. The grittiness of the abandoned mechanic's garage looked and smelled and felt irreverent. It certainly didn't seem like a place where people would go for church. But as Evans stood in the middle of that garage, grime clinging to the bottoms of his shoes, he knew he had found Fellowship's new home.

Fellowship had been holding services at Canaan Center for about four years. By this time, around three hundred people were attending Fellowship's worship services every Sunday. Even more were listening over the radio. Canaan Center had served its purpose well. But the facility could no longer accommodate Fellowship's growth. A suspected turf dispute also made relocating necessary, in Evans's view. Fellowship was bursting at the seams. It seemed to grow larger each week. Canaan Baptist Church, which owned the community center Fellowship rented for its services, was not experiencing the same kind of growth. Evans believed some leaders at Canaan Baptist Church were concerned Evans was stealing potential members. A. R. Leak, who had rented his funeral home chapel to Evans four years earlier, was chairman of the board of Canaan Center. According to Evans, Leak informed him that Canaan Center board members wanted Evans and Fellowship out of the space. The reason, Evans surmised simply, was jealousy. "I was drawing such a crowd at that time, and it was right next door to the main church." Given the increasingly large numbers Fellowship was drawing each Sunday, it was necessary that Evans find a bigger space anyway.

Evans began scouting possible new locations for Fellowship. He wasn't looking for a permanent space. He just needed a space where Fellowship could worship for a few more years until the congregation could afford to build its own building. Evans again turned to the real estate agent who two years earlier had helped him arrange Fellowship's first radio broadcast with WWCA in Gary, Indiana. The real estate agent told Evans about an abandoned garage on 4621 South State Street, which the owners wanted to sell for $25,000.[1] He thought Evans might revitalize the space for Fellowship's worship services. "I was willing to do it," said Evans, "but you have to have a vision for things. For without a vision, the people perish. And if anyone has a vision, it ought to be the leader."

After inspecting the garage, Evans decided it would be a suitable temporary home for Fellowship. However, he had no illusions about the challenges the new space would present. The garage needed significant renovations. It was dirty and dilapidated. There were fractured pipes and broken windows. The roof leaked. Evans knew turning that grimy garage into a glorious house of worship would take a lot of hard work. But Evans had a vision. He saw a diamond in the rough. "I saw what it could be, what it could become, not what it was. It could become a worship place for us, even though it was leaking from the roof, grease on the floor."

The board members of Canaan Center allowed Evans to continue holding Fellowship's services in the space for several more weeks until some initial work could be done on the garage to prepare it for the congregation's move. Fellowship's members wasted no time. They began the difficult work of transforming that dusty old garage into a house of worship. The task ahead was daunting. But Fellowship's members rolled up their sleeves and got to work. After a few weeks, the garage had been fixed up enough for the congregation to begin meeting there for Sunday-morning services. On June 6, 1954, Evans moved Fellowship to its new home on State Street.[2]

Evans and Fellowship's members settled into the garage. They were proud of all their hard work, but many challenges remained. For instance, the heating system was outdated. To keep warm on cold days, leaders burned coal in a fifty-gallon oil drum. Sometimes the smoke was so thick that worshippers could not see across the room.[3] The most serious challenge was the leaky roof. When it rained, water dripped inside during worship services. The building's plumbing also was in need of repair. There was a drain in the middle of the garage floor, and when it rained, water cascaded to the surface. "Sometimes we'd be in the middle of the service, and we'd hear water coming up from the floor. So we had to move the chairs." But church members soon adjusted to these challenges and, each week, overcame them. "You learn how to survive," Evans said about the experience. "And black folks, we have learned how to survive amazing circumstances and keep on going."

Amazingly, Fellowship's members did not let the challenges of their new church home rob their enthusiasm.

Evans was also more energized than discouraged in the new space. That dingy little garage brought back memories of Evans's humble beginnings in Brownsville, Tennessee. "That reminded me where I came from," he said, recalling the small shack house where he grew up. "Rain would come from the tin roof. We had to move our beds. Wind would come through the windows." Evans believed his time in Brownsville had prepared him to face the hardships he confronted after moving Fellowship into the garage. "Like one season helps another—spring helps summer, summer helps fall, fall helps winter. I thank God for the season in Brownsville. We have seasons in our growth spiritually and physically, . . . so thank God for every season. Use it!"

Each week, the members of Fellowship worked diligently to transform the garage into a sanctuary. They were encouraged by Evans's vision of what Fellowship, in time and by the grace of God, might one day become. Evans credits Fellowship's members back then for believing in his vision and for the countless prayers, sacrifices, and hours of labor each invested to ensure the vision manifested. "I've seen many preachers have great visions for accomplishing something but never became a reality because they couldn't get people to see it or support it." The members of Fellowship not only saw and supported Evans's vision, but they took hold of it, even carried it, into existence. "I never had any opponents," he explained about his members' overwhelming support of his leadership during that season.

Slowly, the members of Fellowship completed one renovation project after the next. "Little by little, you do what's essential," Evans said. Even people outside of Fellowship's membership began helping the congregation renovate the new worship space. Other churches and religious organizations invested considerable support in Evans's vision. These organizations donated furniture and even several instruments. Douglas Funeral Home, for example, donated over five hundred chairs for Fellowship's worship services. With the help of the community and Fellowship's members, Evans oversaw the facelift necessary to turn that grimy garage into a hallowed house of worship. "I put everything into that garage building to give it a worship atmosphere," Evans said. During the next two years, that small, dusty garage slowly transformed. "We turned that thing into a cathedral."

While the transformation of Fellowship's physical worship space was admirable, Evans said the most significant development at Fellowship during that time was the creation of a youth-led children's church. Fellowship's regular Sunday-morning worship service provided adults opportunities to cultivate their spirituality through rituals such as prayer, sacraments, music, and sermons. However, up to this point, youth were not utilized intentionally during Fellowship's worship services. Many youth attended Fellowship because their parents made them. With services geared more toward adults, many youth were often left with nothing to do but sit still and listen—tasks almost impossible for most youth in church. Evans worried children attending Fellowship felt disconnected, uninterested, and, quite honestly, bored during worship services. This was unacceptable to Evans. During his time at Tabernacle Missionary Baptist Church, Evans had learned from Rev. Louis Rawls the importance of providing youth opportunities to serve as leaders on Sunday mornings. Evans, too, believed children should be a vital part of the life of any congregation. "Children need to be a part of your ministry and worship."

To provide children a meaningful worship experience, Evans decided to create a space on Sunday mornings where children had opportunities to participate in similar rituals, discussions, scripture readings, and prayers as the adults in Sunday school and in regular worship services. Creating such a space for youth to express themselves, Evans reasoned, would help make coming to church more meaningful for them. Additionally, Evans was convinced a youth service would attract families in surrounding communities. Parents could rest content in the adult worship service, knowing that their children were well supervised while they also learned general principles of Christianity. Evans utilized the kitchen area behind the choir stand as the location of Fellowship's Junior Church. He appointed a woman named Vivian Franklin as the musician and used various ministers at the church to preach in the form of Bible stories for youth participants. All children between the ages of three and twelve were required to attend Fellowship's Junior Church. Those youth who attended were organized into junior ushers, nurses, and deacons, so they would understand the order and structure of the adult worship service. Evans wanted every child to know about Jesus, so all of them could experience personally what it meant to be a child of God.

Once children turned twelve, they would leave the Junior Church and join the adults for worship in the main sanctuary on Sunday mornings. By the time youth left Junior Church, they were familiar with the language, rituals, and rationale shaping Fellowship's adult worship services. Thus, the Junior Church became an important training ground for Fellowship's youth. It was also an important place of learning for the church leaders who helped facilitate that particular ministry. Some of the ministers who served the Junior Church included Reverends Sylvester Coleman, Arthur Taylor, Ulysses Wright, Grant Kelly, William Reid, William Brooks, Andrew Fondren, Charles Straight, Roosevelt Watkins, Harolyn McIntosh, Dwayne Brown, and Bryan Wilson. Some of the musicians who served the Junior Church include Vivian Franklin, Walterene Johnson, Jill Pilate, Sharon Seals, John Pilate, Estes Evans Jr., and Cherry Fondren. Two of the administrators who served this ministry were Mildred Chandler and Mona Johnson.

The success of the Junior Church and the host of other ministries, programs, and clubs Fellowship developed after moving to the garage at 4621 South State Street was the result of the administrative strength of the church's staff. Evans learned early on as pastor of Fellowship that he needed strong leaders to be successful. He often challenged Fellowship's members about the importance of leadership in the church. "We must remember that everyone who is called to minister is not called to be in the pulpit." But everyone is called to serve, Evans taught. He encouraged his members to think intentionally about how to use their gifts, time, and imaginations in service of the Christian church. "Leading people is hard work. To lead is not easy."

Once members were adequately trained and empowered, Evans could trust them to lead because he had given them a model for ethical leadership. Specifically, he taught his members how to manage power responsibly and with care. "Some people try to use authority or power before they get it. Other people, when they get power, they abuse it. Then some people don't know when they lose power. You can lose your power, abuse your power, or use it before you get it." Equipped with this understanding of the ethics of leadership, members of Fellowship pursued their callings as servant leaders.

After moving Fellowship to the garage, Evans cultivated a group of leaders trained in his model of leadership. These leaders served as secretaries, clerks, and office assistants. Some of the leaders who served at the garage cathedral included Mary Thornton, Lucille Loman, Betty Mullins, Eunice Little, Edith Banks, Beatrice Edwards, Mary Williams, and Celestine West. These leaders were integral to the smooth execution of Fellowship's administrative duties. Women occupied high-ranking roles as administrators at Fellowship in its infancy and in its heyday. The women who first served at Fellowship were instrumental in training and empowering the congregation's leaders—both youth and adults.

It was at the State Street garage that Evans and his staff

developed the administrative infrastructure of Fellowship Missionary Baptist Church. Much of this infrastructure is still in place today. This infrastructure included deacons, trustees, a department of Christian education, a missions department, the youth choir, the children's ministry, clubs and small groups, the kitchen ministry, the radio broadcast, and the staff ministers. This administrative structure was the foundation upon which Fellowship was built.

In many ways, Evans's parents had played a crucial role in teaching him the importance of strong administration. Henry and Estanauly Evans taught their children that a person needs family and supporters to be successful. You cannot do it alone, Evans's parents taught him. His parents' advice about delegation and enlisting others' talents and ideas in service of a larger vision guided Evans as he built Fellowship's administrative foundation.

With strong administrative bones in place, Fellowship was finding its legs. The church continued to experience steady growth. Two years after moving to the garage, Fellowship had a recorded membership of about two thousand people.[4] A little over three hundred people regularly attended Sunday-morning worship services—at least that's how many would comfortably fit in the garage. Fellowship's membership had again outgrown its worship space. Evans once again began searching for a new home for "The Ship" to dock.

Evans learned of a Lutheran church on the 4500 block of South Princeton Avenue that was available for rent. The Lutheran church certainly had enough space to accommodate Fellowship's growing membership. But there was another reason Evans found the Lutheran church so appealing. Adjacent to the church were several acres of vacant property. As Evans gazed upon that grassy vacant lot, he imagined Fellowship's permanent building one day resting on that very site. He was proud of the work Fellowship's members had accomplished to transform that dirty old garage into a beautiful sanctuary. "We were still trying to improve it when we left there. We needed a new roof. We needed new washrooms." Yet even after all the labor invested in his garage cathedral, Evans was still not satisfied. Fellowship had not yet found its permanent home. "You can fix up these old buildings, but they are not a church or a sanctuary. . . . I wanted a church building."

Fellowship purchased the Lutheran church building for $110,000.[5] Evans officially moved the congregation to their new church home on November 15, 1959. It was a historic occasion. A motorcade of almost two hundred cars traveled across the Dan Ryan Expressway to Fellowship's new home. This move marked a major milestone in the congregation's life. For the first time since its organization in 1950, Fellowship would be meeting in an actual church building.

Fellowship thrived in its new home at the Lutheran church. In fact, 1960 marked the beginning of several significant developments in the ministries Fellowship offered. Specifically, Evans expanded a series of social-service programs to meet the needs of people living in the surrounding community. Evans had gleaned the importance of the humanitarian aspect of Christian ministry from his mentor,

Rev. Louis Boddie, who was pastor at Greater Harvest Baptist Church. Service to others, Evans proclaimed regularly, was a fundamental duty of every Christian. In the 1950s, when Fellowship was in its infancy, Evans cultivated a series of ministries designed to provide basic life needs to people struggling to make ends meet. In 1955, Evans began a tradition of distributing Christmas baskets to people in need. In 1956, Evans played a key role in establishing the Institute for Christian Service.[6] However, after Fellowship settled into the Lutheran church in 1959, Evans redesigned Fellowship's ministries to reach beyond the surrounding community out toward people in need throughout the city. What would define each ministry, Evans vowed, was a commitment to serve the people of Chicago.

Gradually, Fellowship's commitment to meeting the needs of Chicago's most vulnerable citizens began to attract the attention of the city's white power brokers. In fact, in 1960, city leaders convened a gathering to formally recognize Evans for his example as a leader in service to the local community. The special ceremony, held in the Sherman Hotel, recognized Evans and Fellowship Missionary Baptist Church collectively as a positive social force that had improved the quality of life for people in Chicago and in surrounding areas.[7] Evans attributed this recognition to Fellowship's radio broadcast. The radio broadcast had not only gotten word out about Fellowship's dynamic music ministry and its mission of service to thousands of people. The broadcast also created a buzz among the city's white political elite, who could not ignore the increasing influence

Evans and Fellowship were beginning to have on Chicag
citizens.

At the time, Evans viewed the public affirmation from
city leaders as the beginning of a journey that would forge
more just and loving relationships between black and white
communities in Chicago. Rose describes Evans's hopeful
sentiments during that ceremony: "As Clay extended his
hand to Mayor Richard Daley and the other city officials, he
truly believed it was a gesture of friendship. In that moment,
when black hand clasped white, he truly believed that at last
a bridge of understanding, acceptance, had been built. Little did he know how soon that hand would be pulled away,
turned against him; how quickly the bridge of trust would
collapse in a heap of broken promises and broken dreams."[8]

Ironically, it was Evans's belief in the inherent dignity
of every person that would swiftly cast him out of favor
and fellowship with the city's white political elite. It was
no secret that Evans was a supporter of civil rights. The
time Evans spent under the mentorship of Rev. Louis Boddie instilled in him an unapologetic mission of advocating
for the least, the last, and the left out of a society. As far as
Evans was concerned, a church that remained silent when
any person's rights had been violated—whether that person
was black or not—was a church that was not embodying the
work or witness of Jesus Christ.

Though Evans spent the decade spanning 1950 to 1960
developing social-service programs at Fellowship, he was
not satisfied the church had done enough to confront racial
discrimination against African Americans in Chicago and

beyond. There was more that could be done, he insisted, to show that black lives mattered and to reveal how celebrating the beauty of black life created opportunities for all citizens in a community to see more clearly the dignity of all lives. There was a need, Evans believed, for Fellowship to be more invested in African Americans' struggle for civil rights in Chicago. Therefore, Fellowship pressed on, full speed ahead of many of the city's black congregations in its mission to challenge racism in Chicago loudly and publicly. Evans began the work of instilling in Fellowship's members the importance of confronting the evils of racism and the inhumanity of racists. He accomplished this effectively through the church's music. Interestingly, both scholars and historians have neglected to analyze adequately the links between Fellowship's music and its activism between the 1960s and 1970s. Fellowship's music provided a rich cultural and spiritual well from which African Americans could draw strength and inspiration for the journey toward a more just and hopeful shore.

NOTES

1. Fellowship Missionary Baptist Church, "Our History," http://fellowshipchicago.com/history/.

2. Fellowship Missionary Baptist Church, "Our History."

3. Dorothy June Rose, *From Plough Handle to Pulpit: The Life Story of*

Rev. Clay Evans, a Man with a Mission (Warminster, PA: Neibauer, 1981), 40.

4. Rose, *From Plough Handle to Pulpit*, 41.

5. Rose, *From Plough Handle to Pulpit*, 41.

6. Rose, *From Plough Handle to Pulpit*, 41–42.

7. Rose, *From Plough Handle to Pulpit*, 42–43.

8. Rose, *From Plough Handle to Pulpit*, 43.

12

SINGING IN ZION

I enjoyed directing the choir, because I allowed God to direct me, and I directed people. And there we met—the Spirit, me, and the people. And the results were great!

—Lou Della Evans-Reid

BETWEEN 1959 AND THE 1990s—By the time Evans moved Fellowship to its present location at 4543 South Princeton Avenue in November 1959, the choir boasted well over one hundred people. Evans's sister Lou Della had served as the choir director for over ten years and managed to corral a diverse group of singers. Those with music backgrounds and those with little or no formal music training were all singing together. Not having formal auditions made it much easier to grow the choir. Anyone serious about singing, even if not a strong singer, was welcome to join the choir. Evans gave Lou Della absolute power in how she led the choir. "What she said was law and gospel," Evans said, referring to the trust he extended to his sister. This freedom to direct Fellowship's choir as she saw fit, Lou Della said, was one of the main reasons for the choir's success. "He valued whatever music I selected or however I handled the choir," she said about Evans. "Most of all, he wanted a Spirit-filled choir."

When Fellowship moved into the former Lutheran church, the choir was already known throughout Chicago for its high-energy, Spirit-filled singing. "The atmosphere was so good," Lou Della said about the music during Fellowship's worship services. "The spirit was so high." Every Sunday, Fellowship's choir fascinated and inspired those who attended worship. Usually, at the beginning of the worship service, the choir marched into the sanctuary, singing a hymn, which could be either slow or upbeat. After all choir members were in the choir stand, there was a morning hymn, which also could be slow or upbeat. Next would come a faster-paced gospel song. "Upbeat with some good words that you think they might be waiting for," Lou Della said, referring to the congregation. "Something to start them off on a new week." During the offering, when people actually got up out of the pews to place their financial contributions in church offering plates, an upbeat song was usually played. The song sung right before the sermon varied in style and tempo. "It can be a good hymn, a good song that will lead him [Evans] up to where he needs to start," Lou Della said. "You had to feel your audience and how things are. It depends. Usually it was a slower type of song, one that speaks to the soul of the people."

No matter how slow or fast the tempo of the musical

selections on any given Sunday, Fellowship's choir found constant encouragement in Lou Della's seemingly endless enthusiasm and insatiable passion. Her personality helped inspire the choir's effervescent personality. Sometimes, when one song would end, the choir, feeling particularly moved by the atmosphere of worship, would launch spontaneously into a song that had not been rehearsed or planned for that particular Sunday service. "They were never ready to stop," Lou Della said, laughing. "He [Reverend Evans] might throw up his hand [signaling to the choir that they needed to finally stop singing]. We enjoyed singing. The choir was ministering. And we enjoyed ministering, giving the gifts that God had given back to him."

In the mid-1960s, Evans received a compelling proposal from Chess Records owner Leonard Chess to broadcast Fellowship's worship services on Chess's all-black twenty-four-hour radio station, WVON. Surprisingly, at the time, other than WVON there was no radio station in the city that catered solely to African Americans twenty-four hours a day. In the spring of 1962, Chess and his brother Phil had purchased WHFC 1450 AM from Richard Hoffman, a former Illinois congressman, for one million dollars.[1] Located on South Kedzie Avenue in Cicero, WHFC was just a few miles away from Chess Recording Studios on Michigan Avenue.[2] After purchasing WHFC, the Chess brothers renamed the station WVON, which stood for "Voice of the Negro."

The purchase and naming of WVON were brilliant business maneuvers. Given the high number of African Americans living within the short range of WVON's 1,000-watt frequency signal—which reached the entire Black Belt—it made sense to establish a radio station for African Americans exclusively twenty-four hours a day. Historian Timuel Black recalls that the high concentration of blacks in the city's Black Belt made it necessary to create such "parallel institutions."[3] WVON first aired on April 1, 1963. A year later, a *Billboard* article published March 28, 1964, stated that WVON ranked second in ratings, with Chicago's powerhouse WLS leading.[4] In May 1964, the Pulse Ratings, an independent Chicago radio rating service, recorded WVON having between 44 and 48 percent of black listeners daily.[5]

After the radio station's immediate success, Chess began searching for several prominent black pastors with large congregations and mass choirs to broadcast over WVON's airwaves. Leonard Chess was interested in Evans's voice because it represented the southern Delta sound Chess's target audiences in Chicago were beginning to crave. By the mid-1940s, consumer tastes had begun to move away from the classic 1930s-rooted blues styles toward the West Coast jump blues and downhome Delta blues. Thus, Leonard Chess began looking for people reared in the rural South whose musical sensibilities had been profoundly shaped by the southern Delta gospel blues style. Fellowship's choir, anchored by Evans's bluesy voice, embodied exactly the kind of distinctly southern worship culture that was representative of the changing tastes in Chicago music in the early 1960s.[6] Though not a traditional blues singer, Evans had grown up a stone's throw from Mississippi and Memphis, where the Delta blues had spread like wildfire. During his years in Brownsville, Evans had been steeped in the music and cultural tradition Chess was trying to market to the masses of black southerners living in Chicago. The Delta blues exuded unmistakably through Evans's singing and preaching. Evans's voice had exactly the musical quality Chess was seeking.

The primary advantage black ministers like Evans stood to gain from having their services broadcast live on WVON was an instant audience comprising most of the black population living on Chicago's South and West Sides. Chess's invitation to Evans to broadcast Fellowship's church services on WVON would extend the reach and influence of Evans's ministry and Fellowship's choir significantly. In addition to Evans, Chess approached Evans's friends the Rev. Clarence Cobbs, pastor of First Church of the Deliverance, and Rev. Louis Boddie, pastor of Greater Harvest Baptist Church. Chess discussed with Evans, Cobbs, and Boddie the benefits of broadcasting their services on WVON. Chess's agenda was obvious. He hoped the participation of prominent black pastors like Evans, Cobbs, and Boddie would increase his listening audience and consequently draw more attention and business to his radio station. "He felt like if he had us, others would want to be on there," Evans explained.

Evans jumped at the opportunity and reached an arrangement with Chess and WVON to broadcast Fellowship's worship services. "I was glad about it," Evans said, noting that WVON had already garnered significant credibility among Chicago's black community. "Man, I was hot stuff back then!" Evans exclaimed about the local and national attention Fellowship received after being broadcast on WVON. Once Fellowship's services were broadcast on WVON, increasing numbers of African Americans who had not yet heard Evans or his choir sing were introduced to the vibrant, soul-stirring music ministry of Fellowship Missionary Baptist Church.

Mary Stinson began singing in Fellowship's choir in 1958, when she was eighteen. "It was a wonderful time for me," Stinson said about being a teenager singing in Fellowship's choir, "because I was a young lady, and I was given the opportunity. I was one of the lead soloists. They found out that I could sing." Stinson had moved to Chicago the previous year, in 1957, from Mobile, Alabama. Shortly after Stinson's move to Chicago, her sister also moved to the city from Alabama and began attending Fellowship, which then was located at the garage at 4621 South State Street. Throughout 1957, Stinson worshipped regularly at Fellowship. But she did not join the church officially until 1958. When Stinson first started attending Fellowship, the radio broadcast was at 4:00 p.m. This meant that on Sundays, Stinson was often at Fellowship the entire day. "I enjoyed every minute of it. I was there from Sunday school all the way up to the broadcast." Stinson also attended church events at Fellowship throughout the week, sang in concerts, and listened to musical greats like Sam Cooke and others perform at the church. She was at Fellowship almost every day of the week.

"It was enjoyable. Not only that, not too many people then had cars. My sister and I took the bus. We spent just as much money going to church as we did to work."[7]

Stinson recalled the many adventures Fellowship's choir had as they performed concerts across the country and even overseas. Church members who weren't even in the choir often accompanied the choir on their domestic excursions. The church provided buses that people in the caravan rode for free. Those road trips, Stinson said, were often the only times many of Fellowship's members were able to travel for leisure. "That's the only reason some people got their vacation. It was cheaper to go on the buses. We stayed in nice hotels. Almost everyone took their families with them." Once the choir was invited on an all-expenses-paid singing tour in Italy. "That was something else. . . . They paid our way to come to Italy. The entire choir!" The choir spent nineteen days in Italy, singing at well-known churches there. Stinson praised Evans for exposing members of Fellowship to the world outside of Chicago. "Some of us had never been nowhere or done anything. It was really good for the people," she said. Stinson sang in the choir faithfully for forty-two years. "It was wonderful. We did all types of songs—anthems, hymns, gospel. It was one of the highlights of my life," Stinson recalled.

Another Fellowship singing legend, Loretta Oliver, began singing in Fellowship's choir in 1985. She had been tagging along with Fellowship during its summer concert tours to different parts of the country. "I was a visitor, and after I went so many times, I just felt like I need to be here,"

Oliver said. After formally joining the choir, Oliver became one of the lead soloists. As a soloist, she traveled with the choir on various tours across the United States and abroad. In 1998, she traveled with Evans and Fellowship's choir to Paris, France. "That was when the song 'I've Got a Testimony' came out," Oliver explained, "and I went with him to sing that." In 2011, after twenty-six years singing in Fellowship's choir, Oliver resigned. "I felt that my time was up in the choir and I had set the pace for many others, and there were not very many seniors left in the choir. I was one of the only ones doing lead singing, and so I felt like I was pulling the wagon for everybody." Oliver enjoyed her years singing in Fellowship's choir. The energy during morning worship back then, she said, was almost indescribable. "Well, it's a wonderful feeling when you have an audience that's interested in hearing you and if they can just kind of encourage you as you're singing. . . . The more you're encouraged, the more you feel like singing. . . . If you encourage me, I'm going for the gold. If you don't encourage me, I will hurry up and sit down," she said jokingly.

Lou Della marveled at the extraordinary privilege she was extended to stand where she stood as Fellowship's choir director, surrounded by hundreds of Spirit-filled singers and each Sunday witnessing those faithful voices in full, syncopated musical flight. "I felt like I was in heaven! My heart was rejoicing to see all of us come together in unity. There we are, worshipping God in spirit and in truth. . . . The Lord was there. He was there!" The choir's energy was contagious. Many who heard Fellowship's choir on the radio or on their record albums were compelled to visit Fellowship to experience the magic in person. "They came to see what it was all about," Lou Della said, "and they wanted to be a part of us." She elaborated further: "In most black churches, music is a vital component in the worship experience. If you got a good choir, a good musician with a good choir, and you got good preaching, more than likely your church is going to grow. People will draw to good singing and good preaching. And that was one of the things that caused us to grow, I think. I'm not boasting, but I'm just making a statement."[8]

Pharis Evans, Evans's brother and one of the organizing members of Fellowship, attributed the choir's success and growth to the great musicians who played there. "We always tried to get musicians to work hand in glove with Lou Della," he said. "Different ones. Good musicians. And by getting good musicians and with Lou Della's spirit, the choir just left the three or four that it was [in 1950] and went to twenty, thirty, eighty, ninety and just kept growing."

In 1965, a woman connected with Chess Records approached Evans about recording an album. "Back then, Leonard was hungry for black artists," Evans explained. The prospect of recording an album was exciting indeed. But Evans was becoming busier and busier as Fellowship's senior pastor. His burgeoning congregation required additional pastoral attention. There were more people to counsel, more families to visit, and more funerals and weddings to officiate. Evans was stretched, with little time for additional commitments, but he loved the idea of recording an album of Fellowship's music, featuring the choir and much of his own singing. "I didn't want to ever stop my singing thing, because that was the first thing I did religiously that was noticeable," Evans said. So he and the choir began the grueling work of recording. Fellowship's first album, *Room at the Cross*, was named after one of its songs, which would become a signature song that defined and extended the voice of Rev. Clay Evans worldwide. The album would be the first of over thirty during Evans's fifty years as Fellowship's pastor.

When Fellowship started recording albums, choir members had to travel to the music studio producing the album. "For many years, we went to the studio," Lou Della explained. "We had buses and took the people to the studio." Typically, Fellowship's choir could record an album in several recording sessions, each lasting a few hours. "We might have to go twice and stay three or four hours and maybe longer." As the choir grew, it became more difficult to record in a recording studio. When the choir increased to several hundred people, all albums were recorded at Fellowship. "Mostly when we got to two hundred people, we were doing recordings at the church. . . . The truck would come in and bring everything we needed," Lou Della recalled. Recording sessions at the church usually went smoothly. Lou Della made sure of that. "Most of the time, we could do it in one setting," she boasted. But there were times, she admitted, when the choir had to start a song over two or three times. "It was just how well we could do each song," she said.

Evans's voice was the centerpiece of many of the choir's recorded albums. The uniqueness of her brother's voice, Lou Della said, connected well with listeners:

We did many LPs, and of course we featured him [Evans] on there. His voice was his voice—scratchy but passable. It's not altogether how good a voice. It's what you got *in* the voice that you can produce. . . . And that's what made his songs. It's what he had in the voice, what came out of the voice, how he was able to portray Christ in the voice. . . . That's what put the songs over. So we dare not do any LP or any recording without him. And that's all you need, to have somebody behind you pushing you. And the choir was right there with him. And good musicians gave him what he wanted and had the choir right there.[9]

Fellowship's recorded albums, along with its radio (and starting in 1977 television) broadcasts, gave Rev. Clay Evans and the two-hundred-voice Fellowship Missionary Baptist Church choir a global platform. By 1980, Fellowship's music had a faithful international audience. At that time, the choir was touring twice a year, one stateside tour and one overseas tour.

By the late 1980s, the choir was receiving invitations to sing in Europe. One invitation came after a Swedish singing group, whose members had heard one of Fellowship's gospel albums, traveled to Chicago for one of the stops on their US tour. While in Chicago, the members of the group attended a worship service at Fellowship. Having already listened to Fellowship's music on its recorded albums, they were anxious to meet Evans and hear Fellowship's choir in person. After that worship service, the Swedish singing group extended an invitation to Evans and his choir to perform at a gospel festival in Sweden. Evans accepted. In 1988, Evans and ninety members of the choir boarded a plane, almost filling it completely, for Sweden. For most of the choir members, that trip was their first time traveling internationally. Rev. Dr. Harolynn McIntosh, who joined Fellowship on January 23, 1983, accompanied the choir on the trip to Sweden. McIntosh recalled the experience, saying, "We had an album entitled *When the Spirit Moves*. Everywhere people came out because they had little encounters with gospel music. There are some choirs from there who always fellowship with us when they come to the United States. At one small church, someone had ridden a horse [and buggy], and he too had his head through the window, swinging it to the beat of our soulful gospel."[10] Michael Shaw, Fellowship's pianist at the time, also traveled with the choir to Sweden. "Reverend Evans exposed his people to so much stuff," Shaw said.[11]

In 1998, about one hundred of Fellowship's members traveled to Israel and Egypt. The eleven-day trip included stops in Memphis and Cairo and at the pyramids. Interestingly, less than two weeks after Fellowship returned to the United States, massive fighting erupted in some of the areas members of the congregation had visited. During the trip to Israel, McIntosh said, "Reverend Evans baptized ninety-seven people in the Jordan River, where we saw foot-long fish swimming. One sister became overcome by the Spirit and shouted Reverend's left pool shoe off. One of the deacons offered to help. Reverend replied, 'Naw, man, these are my people; got to do this, got to do this.' He genuinely loved and cared for us. Shepherds, true shepherds are rare."[12]

For five decades, Evans's ministry and Fellowship's choir captivated audiences throughout Chicago, the country, and the world. The live radio broadcast and the choir's recorded albums did much to increase Fellowship's prominence. But it was the church's television broadcasts beginning in the late 1970s that catapulted Fellowship into the stratosphere of national and international fame. Fellowship's worship services were taped on Sunday and aired the following Saturday on channel 28. After seeing the broadcast, many were compelled to attend Fellowship the next morning for Sunday services. Additionally, the television broadcast exposed many white audiences to African American worship for the first time. "I was one of the first [black pastors] to get on television here in Chicago," Evans claimed.

Broadcasting was Evans's niche. Whether radio or television, Evans mastered the use of media in ministry during his time as senior pastor of Fellowship. "That's a great, great ministry [radio and television]. Find your niche. Some fellows are not broadcast ministers," he confidently acknowledged. Evans admonished, "Find out what the Spirit wants you to do. It doesn't mean you're not being successful because you don't rouse people. Just do what the Lord has called you to do. I feel like this was what the Lord wanted me to do, and I didn't want to rebel." Much like Fellowship's radio broadcast thirty years earlier, the church's television broadcast proved an effective marketing tool. "The media was my thing, whether it was recording, radio, or television that reached beyond the four walls. That was my way of reaching [the masses] and connecting with them. It costs you money. But being a Christian costs you also if you don't let your light shine," Evans declared.

Many great musicians forged a pathway that aided Evans's success in ministry. Musicians who served in the early days of Fellowship's music ministry created a foundation on which future generations could build. Musicians such as Willie Webb, Milton Brunson, Albert Goodson, Frederick Young, and Charles Walker all paved the way for younger musicians like Michael Shaw and Royal "Mickey" Warren. Shaw, minister of music at Victory Missionary Baptist Church in Las Vegas, Nevada, served as Fellowship's pianist from 1974 to 2000. Shaw began attending Fellowship in 1962. When he joined the youth choir, Warren was its director. Both were teenagers at the time and talented musicians. Shaw played the piano, and Warren the organ. Since Shaw and Warren had grown up together at Fellowship, they were familiar with each other's musical talents.

Evans had high expectations for Fellowship's musicians. He needed musicians who would build upon the music ministry's success. In a bold move, Evans decided to hire both Shaw and Warren as Fellowship's primary musicians in 1974. Given the size of the choir, Evans's decision stunned many of Fellowship's members. In the past, Fellowship's musicians had been older and more seasoned. Hiring two teenagers to lead the church's 250-member choir was a decision Shaw said "was totally unheard of."[13] Together, Warren and Shaw would carry Fellowship's music ministry from the 1970s into the new millennium.

Evans always kept several talented musicians lined up and ready to serve Fellowship. "Good musicians came my way, and I employed them," he said. He also admitted that sometimes his leadership style created a revolving door for musicians at Fellowship. "I used to have a bad habit. I would fire you in a minute." Looking back, Evans acknowledged the flaws of his often-short temper as a pastor. But he remained unapologetic about the standard of excellence he expected from all Fellowship's employees, especially the church's musicians. "Musicians, sometimes they are just lazy. They came in late. I considered myself a real pastor who kept my finger on the pulse of everything. I believe in pastoring. That's the way a doctor would examine you. They would take your pulse. I watch what people say from a spiritual point of view," Evans explained about his style of pastoral leadership. Being Fellowship's organizing pastor, Evans felt a tremendous burden to make sure the church functioned according to his vision. Thus, firing a musician was always a complex emotional process. "I was wrong sometimes," Evans admitted, explaining the internal tension he often experienced when he relieved a musician of duty at Fellowship. "I was very sensitive to my church being what I felt like it could be."

Many celebrated musicians and singers helped make Fellowship a world-renowned ministry during Evans's time as pastor. However, Evans said the great esteem the choir gained during his pastorate was because of his sister, Lou Della Evans-Reid, who trained and directed Fellowship's choir from 1950 until 2000. Dr. Johari Jabir describes Lou Della Evans-Reid as a pioneer who has not received the recognition she deserves for the feats she accomplished as director of Fellowship's world-famous choir:

If Rev. Clay Evans was the architect and engineer of "The Ship" then it is only fitting to acknowledge the conductor of "The Ship," Evan's sister, Lou Della Evans Reid. The music at the "ship" was known for its pulsating swing and bluesy coloring of hymns, spirituals, and modern gospel. Under the direction of Dr. Evans-Reid the choir generated a collective sense of swing and sway that mirrored the style of Louis Jordan. "Mama Lou" as she is known has an obvious flare for turning a mass choir into a big band orchestra as most of the up-tempo arrangements recorded by the Fellowship Choir find the sopranos mimicking the high-horn stylings of Ellington band members Rex Stewart and Cootie Williams. During their tenure, attending a service at the "ship" entail[ed] your getting on board but it *also* insisted that you get involved. This means that the blues was part of the church's sacred technology of collective affirmation. And this was no coincidental recreational pleasure, though it did indeed satisfy the need for pleasure. But in the historical context of Rev. Evans' social activism African Americans were drawn to the far reaching ministry of the "ship" because they sought the antiseptic quality of the blues that took place aboard the "ship."[14]

Lou Della's tenacity inspired Fellowship's choir to be the force it was on Chicago's South Side, throughout the country, and around the world. However, equally important to the choir's success, if not more important, was the close, personal connections choir members cultivated with one another over the years. From the very beginning, Lou Della explained, she taught choir members to think of the choir as a family. "I knew all of the choir members," she said. "You need to know them individually. And that's important." Before every rehearsal on Thursday evenings, Lou Della would gather the choir for a prayer meeting. "We had prayer meeting first for the church, and then after the prayer meeting, we had rehearsal. So there you got it—prayer meeting and then rehearsal. First things first. And God grew our choir. It just started growing."

Lou Della often assumed a pastoral role when interacting with choir members. She called members on the phone when they were not present for rehearsal on Thursday evenings or for worship on Sunday mornings. "Why aren't they coming? What are their circumstances? . . . We'd find that the choir members would have problems like everyone else." Whenever a choir member was sick or had a relative pass away, Lou Della would have every choir member write personal messages on a card for that person. "And if a member of the choir passed away and they were an active member, oh, we had some kind of a funeral!"

No matter how large the choir grew, one dynamic never changed: "It was a family. I kept telling them, 'We are a family.'" And like in all families, there were times when family members were in need of correction. "There was time when you had to be stern," she admitted about her role as choir director. "But there was a time and place for everything. . . . Sometimes you have to be flexible even with the rule." And if there was ever a significant conflict within the choir or if Lou Della discerned that there was a particular weight burdening the choir, she would name the issue publicly and then call the choir to participate in corporate prayer or other healing rituals celebrated within the church's theological and doctrinal traditions. "I'll tell them, 'We need a fast.'" Lou Della believed this sense of togetherness, especially in chaotic or painful times, enabled Fellowship's choir to ascend to such high heights. "The choir enjoyed what they were doing. They reached out to me, and we all reached up to God. We enjoyed what we were doing."

In celebration of her seventy-fifth birthday in 2005, Lou Della, who had already retired as Fellowship's choir director, recorded an album with the church's choir. As part of her birthday celebration, Fellowship's choir planned a reunion concert. On Friday, July 8, 2005, the choir rehearsed at Fellowship. "Everybody was excited," she said. "All these people had come in that had not been around. . . . The choir stand was full and running over. We had at least three hundred choir members." Fred Nelson, the musician for the reunion concert, felt that the moment was too special for it not to be recorded. Nelson and Lou Della agreed that the choir's concert that Sunday should be recorded as a CD. In the past, when Fellowship's choir had recorded an album, Lou Della would sometimes stop the choir in the middle of a song if she felt the quality of their performance was not high enough. They would regroup, compose themselves, and start the song over. But amazingly, during the reunion choir's concert, there weren't any restarts. "That afternoon, we recorded straight through," Lou Della said proudly. "That was one of the best recordings we'd ever done!"

Reflecting back over the years, Evans expressed his awe at the great work God did through Fellowship's choir. Though Evans is proud of the work the choir produced, he is most proud of the choir's long and distinguished career singing the songs of Zion. "To maintain it as long as we did was unique. You see preachers and stars rise up. They're in the sunlight for a little while, and they're gone," he pondered. That wasn't the case with Fellowship. As a long-time soloist in the choir, Stinson exclaimed, "We weren't playing! We were in it to sing!"[15]

NOTES

1. "New Station WVON Aimed at Negro Marked Debuts Monday," *Chicago Defender*, March 30, 1963. Lejzor "Leonard" and Fiszel "Phil" were born in Poland in 1917 and 1921, respectively. In 1928, the impoverished family immigrated to the United States, changed their name from Czyz to the Americanized "Chess," and settled in a Russian Jewish neighborhood of Lawndale. The Chess brothers eventually began a number of ventures in Chicago, including operating liquor stores, running bars, and hiring musicians for their establishments—the largest being the Macomba Lounge on 39th Street and South Cottage Grove. The Macomba Lounge provided a critical venue for up-and-coming black musical talent. Jennifer Searcy, "The Voice of the Negro: African American Radio, WVON, and the Struggle for Civil Rights in Chicago" (PhD diss., Loyola University, 2003), p. 31, paper 688, http://tinyurl.com/y7gpcxya; Rich Cohen, *Machers and Rockers: Chess Records and the Business of Rock and Roll* (New York: W. W. Norton, 2004), 23–25; Gerald E. Brennan, "Leonard Chess: Record Company Owner," *Enclyclopedia.com*, http://tinyurl.com/yaqgnysv.

2. Searcy, "Voice of the Negro," 68; Wesley South, interview by Julieanna Richardson, videocassette, July 18, 2000, HistoryMakers African American Video Oral History Collection, Chicago; *Broadcasting*, 1959 Yearbook Issue, p. A-276.

3. Timuel Black, interview by Melody Spann-Cooper, January 26, 2016, WVON Midway Broadcasting Corporation Studios, Chicago.

4. David Whiteis, "Not So Smooth Operator," *Chicago Reader*, January 18, 2001, http://tinyurl.com/ybcguam2. Also see Kit O'Toole, *Michael Jackson FAQ: All That's Left to Know about the King of Pop* (Milwaukee: Backbeat, 2015). O'Toole mentions the *Billboard* article at the beginning of chapter 3, "If It's in the Stars, They're Surely on My Side: How the Jackson 5 Were Really Discovered."

5. Phil Chess, interview by Michael McAlpin, transcript, ca. 1994, Michael McAlpin Collection, Archives of African American Music and Culture, Bloomington, IN.

6. John Collis, *The Story of Chess Records* (New York: Bloomsbury, 1998), 24.

7. Stinson, phone interview by author, 2013, Chicago.

8. Lou Della Evans-Reid, interview by the author, 2012, Fellowship Missionary Baptist Church, Chicago.

9. Lou Della Evans-Reid, interview.

10. Rev. Dr. Harolynn McIntosh, written response solicited by author, 2012.

11. Michael Shaw, phone interview, by author, 2013, Chicago.

12. McIntosh, interview.

13. Shaw, interview.

14. Dr. Johari Jabir, e-mail interview by the author, 2012, Chicago.

15. Stinson, interview.

13

THE TEMPEST IS RAGING

I was persecuted and talked about. "Clay, you're a fool . . . joining up with Dr. King. You're a fool. We're going to mess you up." I figured they couldn't mess me up no more than the Lord could.

—Rev. Clay Evans (2011)

I can understand losing favor with city leaders. But I could never understand religious men, spiritual men, pulling away from their brother who entertained a man who was more after Christ than most of these [pastors] because Martin Luther King had a social gospel.

—Minister Louis Farrakhan (2012)

SUNDAY, JULY 4, 1965—Two young civil rights activists drove down a Chicago highway, listening to the car radio. Educated and passionate, both were eager to become more involved in the national movement for civil rights that Dr.

Martin Luther King Jr. and others were leading. On this particular Sunday, Jesse Louis Jackson and Henry O. Hardy were on their way to church. The car radio blasted local church services on Chicago's WVON radio station. Suddenly, a soulful voice crooned over the radio. It was Rev. Clay Evans, singing "I Must Tell Jesus." Jackson sat up in the car seat. He looked wide-eyed at the car radio, listening as Evans's voice roared on. "I said, 'Where is that, and who is that?'" Jackson recalled.[1] Hardy responded, "That's Reverend Evans."

That fortuitous day is etched in Jackson's memory. "It was July 4, 1965. I shall never forget it. We diverted from where we were going to come to Fellowship to hear Reverend Evans." Jackson and Hardy arrived at Fellowship shortly before the worship service. They requested to speak with Evans. Within a matter of minutes, the two were escorted into Evans's office. Evans remembered that first encounter with Jackson vividly. "He fell on that couch as if he had been knowing me all those years," Evans recalled. "He had on some high-top shoes. I never will forget it—just making himself comfortable. From that time on, the Lord knitted us together like Jonathan and David. There was something about him. We just clicked. A few Sundays after that, he joined the church."

On the property outside Fellowship, an assortment of construction vehicles and other equipment rested conspicuously. After a few years in the Lutheran church Fellowship had purchased, the church had outgrown the space. Often, standing-room-only crowds filled the church, the basement, and even spilled over onto the sidewalk outside.[2] Evans had decided it was finally time for Fellowship to build its own permanent building from the ground up. Between 1962 and 1963, Evans initiated a congregational campaign to raise the necessary funds to begin construction. Evans impressed upon Fellowship's members that the only way to secure a loan for the building project was to demonstrate to loan officers that Fellowship was a safe and worthy investment. Sure enough, Evans's people responded. Fellowship raised about $150,000 and began petitioning for a loan. In particular, Evans would pitch a loan for a block-long complex that would be annexed to the building in which the congregation was currently meeting. The proposed campus would include a parking lot, a sanctuary, and an education, recreation, and administrative building to house staff offices, classrooms, boardrooms, a cafeteria, and a fellowship hall. The cost of the entire construction project was around $500,000.[3] In 1963, white bankers promised Fellowship a loan to begin construction. The loan was a symbol of the potential partnership between black and white communities in Chicago.[4]

On Sunday, September 23, 1964, Reverend Evans and over 2,500 of Fellowship's members celebrated the official groundbreaking ceremony of the church's building project. It was a joyous occasion. The ceremony was the evidence of fourteen years of faithful partnership between pastor and people. The ceremony demonstrated that the bond between Reverend Evans and the people of Fellowship remained strong—and in fact was made stronger—in moments of

adversity. Evans saw Fellowship's groundbreaking ceremony as a hopeful moment regarding the problem of race.
After all, he thought, the loan the city had just granted
Fellowship to build was evidence that leaders representing
both races were acting in good faith. Certainly injustice
existed, he acknowledged, but progress was being made.
Fellowship's building project gave him every reason to
believe nonconfrontational diplomacy could prevail where
race was concerned. Therefore, while Evans cared about
the civil rights demonstrations exploding throughout the
United States, he was not actively involved in the movement at the time.[5]

Given the scale of Fellowship's building campaign, Evans
divided the construction into two phases. The first phase
involved the construction of Fellowship's main campus and
administration building. The second and final phase of the
project involved building Fellowship's new sanctuary. Each
week, construction crews moved dutifully throughout the
building site. Large machines hauled loads of steel and concrete. Workers mixed fresh cement and laid the appropriate
foundations. After the first phase of the project was completed, phase two began on schedule and progressed with
few problems. It didn't take long to see progress on Fellowship's new sanctuary. Large steel beams jutted toward
the sky from a concrete foundation, connecting horizon-
tally here and there, forming the steel skeleton of Fellowship's new worship space. Each time Evans looked upon
those steel beams, he felt overwhelming pride. All the sacrifice, sweat, and patience endured during the previous six-

teen years had begun to pay off. After a series of exoduses and processions from one temporary location to the next for almost two decades, Evans's dream of a permanent home was almost a reality.

About this same time, a young Baptist preacher from Atlanta, Georgia, was leading a national movement for civil rights. This preacher, four years younger than Evans, had achieved great success in the South. His list of accomplishments was long. In 1955, five years after Fellowship's first worship service, this preacher led a successful year-long boycott in Montgomery, Alabama, to dismantle segregation in the city's bus system. In 1963, this preacher wrote a poetic letter from behind the bars of a Birmingham, Alabama, jail, challenging local clergy from every faith tradition and ethnicity to move beyond mere rhetoric and embody the ideals of justice and equality. Several months later, that same preacher stood on the steps of the Lincoln Memorial in Washington, DC, to share with America his dream for racial justice and equality. The following year, in 1964, he was awarded the Nobel Peace Prize for his relentless pursuit of nonviolent direct action as a means of social transformation. Having achieved significant success in the South, Dr. Martin Luther King Jr. turned his sights toward the urban landscape of the industrial North. King decided that the slum conditions plaguing minorities in the urban North were inextricably linked to intentional practices of racism and segregation he had been fighting in the South. The racism in the South was overt. Yet King observed a more covert racism in the North. This more subtle racism blamed minorities for the dangerous and dehumanizing slum conditions in which they lived.

In 1965, Martin Luther King Jr. traveled to Chicago to address the General Synod of the United Church of Christ. On the morning of July 7, King announced in the Palmer House hotel ballroom that he would be spending time in Chicago beginning July 24.[6] He was considering using Chicago as a base to launch a campaign to expose the racism masquerading as equality in the urban North. It was critical that King and the Southern Christian Leadership Conference (SCLC) expose racism as a national illness that affected both rural southerners and urban northerners. King scholar Taylor Branch said, "Unless the movement could establish the race issue was national—not a deviation peculiar to the Bull Connor stereotype—the promise of nonviolence inevitably would shrivel."[7] King and SCLC leaders had considered other northern cities, such as Boston and New York, and West Coast cities including Los Angeles as possible sites to launch a civil rights campaign. However, it was determined that blacks in Boston were too divided. In New York, prominent black leaders had already shown great resistance to King and the SCLC. And Los Angeles was considered too middle class and still reeling from the Watts riots.[8] Thus, King chose Chicago. He had great hopes the successful dramatization of racism in Chicago would ultimately galvanize a sustainable national movement for civil rights.

King wanted to focus the Chicago campaign on poor education for black children and slum conditions in black communities.⁹ The plan was to use the issue of quality integrated education and housing as concrete issues that shed light on larger, systematic injustices in the city. In his writings, King describes the primary agenda of the Chicago Freedom Movement to be "to bring about the unconditional surrender of forces dedicated to the creation and maintenance of slums and ultimately to make slums a moral and financial liability upon the whole community."¹⁰ A vital part of the Chicago Freedom Movement involved King living and working in Chicago during 1966.¹¹ King moved into the city's Lawndale community to learn from residents about their struggles with poverty and slum conditions in the neighborhood.

To be successful in Chicago, King knew he needed the support of local black pastors. He was hopeful black religious leaders in Chicago would welcome him. After all, King felt they shared the common goal of securing fair and equal access to basic civil rights. Thus, King's first order of business in planning the Chicago campaign was to establish relationships with local black pastors. Alliances with these pastors were needed to mobilize black Chicagoans in a movement for social change within the city. However, King learned quickly that gaining support from black pastors in Chicago would not be easy. As he traveled throughout different Chicago communities, seeking support for his campaign, King faced bitter opposition among many black pastors.

While King prepared to launch a civil rights campaign in Chicago, Rev. Clay Evans was serving as president of

Chicago's Baptist Ministers' Conference, the same organization that had tried to ban Evans from membership years earlier after he licensed Rev. Consuella York. Now, as president of the conference, Evans had significant influence among the city's black Baptist ministers. At the same time, Evans's budding friendship with Jesse Jackson helped him reconsider the extent of racism in Chicago. As someone already involved in civil rights activism, Jackson had concrete experience in analyzing social problems and developing strategies for confronting racism within urban settings. Additionally, Jackson's association with King, having marched with him in Selma in 1964, helped persuade Evans of the importance of being actively involved in the struggle for civil rights. Evans spent hours listening to and learning from Jackson's experiences. Jackson pointed out instances of racial discrimination taking place in Chicago. Slowly, Evans's eyes opened to the larger systemic racism at work in Chicago. As Rose concludes, "Inequalities in such vital areas as jobs, education, housing, products, glared so brightly that he wondered how he could have remained blind to them for so long."[12]

Agreeing with Jackson's and King's analysis of the injustices in Chicago, Evans decided to utilize his position as president of the Chicago Baptist Ministers' Conference to secure support for King's cause in the North. Evans convened a meeting of the city's black Baptist ministers to present Operation Breadbasket, King's national initiative to secure jobs, affordable housing, economic development, and other civil rights for African Americans. Evans envisioned this cohort of minsters as the organizing body that would serve as the foundation of King's freedom movement for blacks in Chicago. Evans assembled ministers at True Light Baptist Church, where Rev. B. F. Paxton was senior pastor at the time. Near the end of the meeting, Evans called for a vote of support for King's campaign for better schools and housing for blacks in Chicago. Then all hell broke loose! Jackson was in attendance and recalled that chaotic moment, which he claimed involved Reverend Paxton:

> We brought the idea of Breadbasket to be adopted by the ministers' conference. The minister said, "Don't bring no Martin Luther King program. We want nothing to do with Martin Luther King." Reverend Evans said, "You can vote it down, but you cannot deny a legitimate Baptist ministers' program a chance to be heard. So I will hear the appeal for the support." When the appeal was brought forth, the minister ran and got his gun out of his study and chased all the ministers, chased them out of the church.[13]

Chuck Bowen, a former aide to Mayor Richard M. Daley, recalled a version of the same story told to him by the late Rev. Richard Williams, who was said to have also been present at that fateful meeting. Bowen, paraphrasing Williams's story, described the tension, saying, "This man pulled out his pistol and said, 'No, I mean go right now. And be quick about it!'"[14] Evans, Jackson, and the other gathered ministers retreated from their chairs and filed promptly into the street outside the church. In a January 18, 2011, article in the *Chicago Defender*, Karen Hawkins referenced this alleged conflict. According to Hawkins, Evans said Reverend Paxton "didn't want us to even discuss" the prospect of supporting Dr. King.[15] Looking back on the experience, Evans does not regret being adamant that King's agenda should be heard. "I was the president of the Chicago Baptist Ministers' Conference, and I wasn't going to let anyone tell me I couldn't bring it up. It was my prerogative as president to bring it up and let the conference make the decision."

Evans believed King's presence in Chicago would create an opportunity to address the structural inequalities oppressing the city's African American residents. Having experienced racism in Brownsville, Evans believed supporting King was the right thing to do: "'I had seen so much of it there and I just didn't think it was fair,' Evans said of the inequities he witnessed in his hometown. So he favored King because Evans 'believed in what he did.'"[16]

After the confrontation at True Light Baptist Church, Evans began holding meetings of the Chicago Baptist Ministers' Conference at Fellowship. Every Friday, Baptist pastors, as well as ministers of other denominations who supported Evans and King, gathered at Fellowship to strategize. King and the SCLC implemented Operation Breadbasket in Chicago, and King appointed Jesse Jackson as the head of the Chicago branch. The organization was remarkably effective at securing gains for blacks. In 1966, Operation Breadbasket secured hundreds of jobs for blacks in the dairy, soft-drink, and supermarket industries. Additionally, the organization reached agreements with companies that committed to do business with black banks. During its first eighteen months in Chicago, Operation Breadbasket reportedly opened 2,500 jobs to blacks, worth an estimated $16 million.[17] Operation Breadbasket's activities in Chicago became an impetus for Evans and Jackson to launch Operation PUSH. In fact, Operation PUSH was founded in the basement of Fellowship in 1966, with Evans serving as the organization's founding chairman. In the years following its founding, Operation PUSH became instrumental in securing civil rights victories for blacks in Chicago. "All those economic breakthroughs," Jackson said, "blacks driving milk trucks . . . and getting products and goods and services at stores—all that stuff came out of Fellowship."[18]

Stories about the intense hostility many black pastors in Chicago showed King are now legendary. The alleged gun-wielding pastor was but one of a host of black pastors who wanted nothing to do with King. J. H. Jackson, then pastor of Olivet Baptist Church and also president of the National Baptist Convention, the chief denominational body governing black Baptist churches in the United States at the time, was one of King's staunchest opponents. J. H. Jackson's contempt for King endured even after King's death.[19] After King's assassination in 1968, city leaders in Chicago decided to rename South Park Boulevard as Martin Luther King Drive in his honor. J. H. Jackson's church was located at the corner of South Park and 31st Street. In an act of defiance that is still talked about in black communities in and beyond Chicago today, J. H. Jackson changed Olivet's address from South Park to 31st Street so that his church would not rest along the street renamed after King.

By the time King announced his campaign in Chicago, significant tensions already existed between King and J. H. Jackson. The two had clashed in an epic contest for power within the National Baptist Convention four years earlier. That conflict resulted in J. H. Jackson excommunicating King from the convention.[20] Thus, when King arrived in Chicago in 1965 with plans to launch a movement for civil rights, the tension between King and J. H. Jackson and his many allies in the National Baptist Convention had had four years to burn. Jesse Jackson recalled the coordinated efforts among black clergy to prevent King from gaining ground in Chicago: "It was the first time that Dr. King was meeting resistance by black ministers who were really having press conferences that he should not come to Chicago," Jackson said. According to Bowen, a former aide to Chicago mayor Richard M. Daley, many of the black pastors interpreted King's presence in Chicago as a challenge to their leadership. "And it's not that Dr. King was coming to challenge them," Bowen explained. "He was coming to lead a movement. . . . They didn't want him to gain notoriety in Chicago."[21]

The resistance among black pastors was partly fueled by the resentment they felt about King, an outsider, who was attempting to address problems on their turf. However, circumstances were more complex than a turf war. Minister Louis Farrakhan recalled that some black pastors in the 1960s had been coopted by the city's white power brokers and had previously negotiated backroom financial deals with politicians in exchange for their loyalty. "Those who got their bread and butter not from God, but from nearness to political realities, felt that if they supported Reverend Evans, they would lose favor with Mayor [Richard J.] Daley and the city machine," Farrakhan explained. "And so they opted for the political rather than the spiritual."[22] Such relationships between black ministers and Chicago politicians often evolved out of the financial instability of many black congregations that were trying to expand to accommodate the steady influx of black southern migrants during the mid-1900s. Some black clergy also accepted fees for supporting political candidates.[23]

Blacks in the city were divided on King's Chicago Freedom Movement. For instance, while many black pastors and white politicians opposed King and his presence in Chicago, WVON radio station publicly endorsed King and his civil rights activities. In August 1964, just over a year since its first broadcast, WVON hosted a sleepless sit-in to raise money to support King and SCLC's civil rights efforts in the city. WVON disc jockeys—the Good Guys, as they were affectionately known—set up a trailer on 35th Street and what is now Martin Luther King Jr. Drive, where they hosted broadcasts live, staying up as long as they could without sleep. WVON disc jockey Pervis "The Bluesman" Spann stayed up the longest, logging eighty-seven and a half hours of no sleep. The WVON promotion raised more than $27,000, which was split between Dr. King, the Urban League, and the NAACP.[24]

Former Illinois governor Pat Quinn was in high school when Dr. King was crusading in Chicago. Quinn in 2012 recalled the mixed feelings about King's presence in the city. At a rally at Soldier Field on Sunday, July 10, 1966, excitement was high among the over fifty thousand gathered to hear King speak.[25] On that "very hot day," Quinn remembered of the rally, "hundreds, thousands of people came out." One month later, King marched amid a hostile crowd during the now-infamous Marquette Park march, during which the civil rights leader was hit in the head with a brick. "I remember Dr. King marching in Marquette Park and in Cicero. . . . I think Dr. King was truly surprised that many of the clergy did not welcome him. . . . In fact, they told him to go home. 'You're not needed here.' And that had to be a very difficult day for Dr. King. He had won the Nobel Prize. He had led victory after victory. This was after Selma. This was after the Voting Rights Act and the Civil Rights Act."[26]

Father Michael Pfleger, priest of the Faith Community of Saint Sabina in Chicago, echoed Farrakhan's sentiments that the Chicago political machine orchestrated much of the opposition King experienced from many black pastors. Many city leaders, Pfleger said, had a role in fueling bitterness toward King:

> When Dr. King came to Chicago, there was a great gathering of power that said, "He can't come in here, and he can't have a voice here, and he can't create what he's done in Birmingham or Selma and Atlanta. He can't do that up in Chicago." And not just corporate

and political powers, but church powers. I think we often talk about his run-ins with the former Mayor Daley. . . . But we often don't hear about his run-ins with other prominent black pastors, white pastors, Hispanic pastors in this city, who told him to back off and condemned him for his actions.[27]

Fellowship Missionary Baptist Church was an easy location to which sympathetic pastors on the city's South and West Sides could travel for strategy meetings with King, Evans, and other supporters. "It was a central location and a good one for them to gather there," Evans explained. King, bruised from the unexpected opposition from the city's black clergy, appreciated and accepted Evans's invitation to use Fellowship each week as a base of operations. "He was very grateful that I would open my doors for such a meeting."

Occasionally, Evans said, the tenor of these meetings would reach a fever pitch as leaders' frustrations about internal disagreements or roadblocks city leaders had engineered threatened to sap the movement's momentum. However, Evans recalled, King always remained calm in the chaos. "He was kind of a normal spirit," Evans remembered. "He wasn't a person to get excited. But he was enthusiastic about the cause." For Evans, King's message was timely and easy to embrace. "I respected him and his philosophy." Historian Timuel Black describes the importance of local leaders like Evans introducing King to various communities throughout Chicago. It was through local leaders like Evans that King was able to gain credibility among many of the people for whom his Chicago campaign was trying to secure quality education and safe and affordable housing.

Word eventually got around that Evans had opened Fellowship as a base of operations for King. And while many black pastors' animosity toward King continued to burn, tempers began to flare even hotter among Chicago's white politicians. "City Hall frankly didn't want Dr. King in our city and did everything they could with the clergy to discourage Dr. King from remaining here," Quinn said. Evans's relationships with Mayor Richard J. Daley and the city's religious and political leaders were severely strained after he publicly endorsed King. "I was really between a rock and a hard place," Evans explained. "The president of the National Baptist Convention, J. H. Jackson, didn't like King either. The mayor was against King. The president of the National Baptist Convention was then against me." Evans's stress was overwhelming. "The pressure. Man, I really don't know now how I withstood it and made it." Evans endured constant criticism. The ridicule many had been hurling at King soon began hitting Evans. "I was persecuted and talked about. 'Clay, you're a fool . . . joining up with Dr. King. You're a fool. We're going to mess you up.' I figured they couldn't mess me up no more than the Lord could."

Religious and political leaders made a host of veiled threats, trying to intimidate Evans into withdrawing his support of King. Still, Evans refused to turn his back on his friend. The doors of Fellowship remained open to King and his staff as they strategized how to expose racism in

Chicago. But several days after Evans participated in a march with King through Chicago's streets, he was summoned to a meeting with the white financers who had promised the loan for Fellowship's extensive construction project. Jackson and King attended the meeting with Evans. There Evans was given an ultimatum. He was to withdraw his support of King, or his loan for construction would be stopped.[28] The mortgage broker went on to assert the mayor could stop any structure in Chicago if he wanted.[29] The threat was severe. Much of the work on Fellowship's new sanctuary remained unfinished. Only the foundation and the sanctuary's steel skeleton structure had been completed. Evans had already spent the $150,000 Fellowship had raised to initiate the construction project.[30] If the financers rejected the loan that had been promised, Evans could lose everything he had spent almost twenty years building. He had considered that standing with King might cost him his ministry as Fellowship's senior pastor. That night, Evans told Jackson that there was no decision to be made. He would stand unapologetically with King: "I've always been a free thinker, not an organization man. I believe in Dr. King and all that we're fighting for, so it's partly a matter of principle. But more than anything, Jesse, the Holy Ghost has inspired me to take this stand, to hold fast to my convictions. I have no choice but to obey."[31]

Not long after Evans refused to bow to city leaders' will, all construction of Fellowship's new sanctuary stopped. Building permits were yanked. Banks rescinded and denied current and future loans to finance the project. The construction crews gathered their materials and drove their equipment and vehicles off the construction site. All that remained was the tall, steel skeleton frame of Fellowship's unfinished sanctuary. The message was clear. There would be consequences for standing with King. "Many ministers who were with us had to back off because they didn't want their buildings to be condemned or given citations for electrical work, faulty plumbing, or fire code violations."[32]

Many believed then and now that the sudden halt of construction of Fellowship's sanctuary was indeed a cleverly orchestrated strategy by city leaders who were opposed to Evans's support of King. "There's no question I think it was," Father Pfleger said. "And I think it wasn't just the former [mayor Richard J. Daley]. I think it was the political and the corporate powers that be."[33] Richard M. Daley, the son of the elder Daley and also a former mayor, shares a different view of his father's administration. "I don't know about that," Daley said about his father's involvement in shutting down construction to Fellowship's sanctuary because of Evans's support of King. "But most black ministers did not want him there, [nor did] black politicians, black businesspeople. Because this is their territory; it wasn't his. [King] was from Atlanta. And within the black community, there were big power struggles there. And so it was easy to blame Mayor Daley. Who else are you going to be blame? He's Caucasian. So that was all part of it. But my father knew that. It didn't bother him at all," said the younger Daley.[34]

Unable to obtain necessary building permits and bank loans, Evans could not continue construction to Fellowship's sanctuary. The project would have to stop indefinitely. Evans later remembered with stinging clarity the pain he felt when construction to his new sanctuary halted: "Oh, man, it's indescribable! People laughed at me. People made fun of me." Often, pastors would stand outside the church, waiting for Evans to come outside. When Evans would appear, they would taunt him. Minister Farrakhan recalls his shock at the level of opposition Evans endured from fellow black Christian ministers then: "I can understand losing favor with city leaders. But I could never understand religious men, spiritual men, pulling away from their brother who entertained a man who was more after Christ than most of these [pastors], because Martin Luther King had a social gospel. And that's the gospel of Jesus Christ. Jesus was not always seen in the synagogues. He was seen in the highways and the byways, meeting with the publicans and the sinners and those who were sick and imprisoned and whatnot."[35]

Each day Evans arrived at Fellowship, the unfinished sanctuary haunted him. Some days, he found encouragement in his conviction that he had acted for a righteous cause. Other days, Evans wondered if his conviction had come at too high a price. Was he being a fool? Rev. Dr. Don Sharp recalled just how public the cost of Evans's decision to support King had become within the black community: "Many times, we drove past there and saw those steel beams there," Sharp said. "Clay had this thing about loyalty. And whatever the price, he was willing to pay it for the sake of loyalty."[36]

At the time construction on Fellowship's sanctuary stopped, Rev. Dr. Otis Moss Jr. was living in Cincinnati, Ohio, and serving as the regional representative for the Southern Christian Leadership Conference (SCLC). Moss later recalled Evans's pain in the wake of the city's response to his endorsement of King: "I had a conversation with Reverend Evans years ago. I don't know if he would even remember it now. And he said to me very privately that there were moments when he looked at that unfinished structure and was embarrassed. And I guess this was another way of saying he was also hurt, that doing the right thing—and it was the right thing, it was the prophetic thing—[cost him so much]. It took moral courage to do what he did."[37]

Evans looked at that unfinished steel frame every day for the next seven years. "Now, that was humiliating—to see the frame up there. Fellows really made a thing out of that," Evans recalled. He could not escape that ugly sight. No matter how many positive things occurred at Fellowship, Evans would eventually have to look upon his great unfinished work. "That worked on my nerves. That worked on everything!" However, Evans kept encouraging his congregation to not lose faith, that God would make a way. Fund-raising activities continued. As Dorothy June Rose recalled, each week Evans "preached in the shadow of that silent and eerie steel skeleton, he would remind his people that, 'even in these times of tribulation, the Lord is with us. He has something He wants us to learn.'"[38] Evans often linked Fellowship's struggle symbolically with the biblical narrative of the people of Israel wandering in the desert for forty years after escaping slavery in Egypt. The members of Fellowship, just like their Israelite brothers and sisters, were searching for sanctuary from those harsh realities threatening their dignity and livelihood. "These days are to us what the wilderness was to the children of Israel," he often said. "They will bring us closer to the Lord. We can and we will do for ourselves what we thought only other folk could do for us."[39] Those seven years were indeed a wilderness experience—a time of constant prayer, fasting, tithing, and service, even in the face of mounting disappointment and uncertainty.[40] It was a time of intense labor with little tangible evidence that anything was ever going to change for the better.

Evans and Fellowship emerged triumphantly from the wilderness on December 18, 1971. Rev. Jesse Jackson was able to intervene successfully on behalf his mentor and friend. Jackson approached several banks about approving a loan so Fellowship could finish its sanctuary. According to Evans, Jackson approached Malcolm Bank in downtown Chicago. "Jesse had to cosign with me," Evans recalled. "I didn't have a good reputation at the time, because I was considered a rebel." Not only did Jackson convince the bank to grant the loan, but he also persuaded several denominations to offer assistance. Other pastors underwrote the loan for the rest of the construction. "I'll never forget: . . . seven denominations decided to underwrite it. They took about $75,000 each. . . . So you see, I must be ecumenical," Evans said smiling, emphasizing that, had it not been for the genuine good-will of different denominations, Fellowship would not have completed the construction of its sanctuary. "This puts in perspective the isms that keep current churches separated. That shows the results when you rise above the isms," Evans resolved.

Frederick C. Harris recalls that difficult time in Evans's ministry. Harris, like many others, acknowledges the significant cost Evans endured for standing in solidarity with King. He also testifies about the significance of different Christian denominations joining together to help resuscitate Fellowship's construction project, writing that "only after a group of clergy came together to guarantee the bank loan," could Fellowship finish its new home.[41]

On April 15, 1973, Evans and Fellowship celebrated the completion of Fellowship's sanctuary, which had stood unfinished since 1965.[42] Evans later credited Jesse Jackson as one of the primary people who had helped get the sanctuary's construction back on track. "Really, Jesse brought me into the civil rights movement. He stood with me because he knew I was in trouble." Pfleger said Evans's defiance of city leaders by supporting King had a tremendous impact on the city of Chicago at the time:

I think it was very clear he knew what Dr. King was doing was not only right, it was necessary. It was as necessary in Selma as it was in Chicago. There was this perception that in the North, everything was all right. And that's what they kept wanting to tell him: "You're jumping into things you need to stay out of. We're all right up here." Pastor Evans was very clear in exposing what is not all right. And what really happened by his standing with Dr. King and endorsing Dr. King, I think it took the cover off all the stuff that was not right up here in Chicago. And I don't think we would have had some of the victories we had and the open housing and the marches and the confrontation that we had in Chicago, had it not been for Clay Evans to pull the cover back and say, "Oh, yes, we've got the same sins and the same evils here."[43]

While the backlash Evans and Fellowship endured for supporting King was certainly painful, it was an opportunity for significant learning and growth. "He refused to give up his principles, even for the new church," Jackson said about his mentor. "His friends laughed at him. But his sense of maturity and dignity, and even his theology changed in those seven years." In 2012, Congressman Bobby Rush, inspired by Evans's leadership even in the face of bitter persecution, echoed Jackson's sentiments. For Rush, the period of time Fellowship's sanctuary stood unfinished has significant spiritual and theological meaning:

I still remember that half-built church and the steel beams that had started to turn red with all the rust. And to me, that half-built church was like a metaphor for the unbroken promises that the African American community was suffering under and what the civil rights movement was all about. It represented a defiant determination to not compromise your basic human rights for the ethical disease of surrendering to the power structure. It really was a symbol. It was a testament to the character of Rev. Evans. . . . The unfinished structure actually kind of completed Reverend Evans's construction as a preeminent political and religious leader. Had he not made that stand, then he probably would have wound up being just a singing preacher that everybody liked to hear sing but nobody really, really respected. In the physical world, that structure was incomplete, but in the spiritual world, he had built an edifice that far exceeded what his expectations would have been.[44]

Evans's sister Lou Della expressed similar thoughts about the larger, cosmic implications of Fellowship's unfinished sanctuary and all the events that precipitated the drama:

We had to leave the building for seven years. But God was using that in another way for us. "I need to build you spiritually. I need to make you stronger. You've got some growing to do." . . . But we know that it was God that took us through it and then gave us the say so: "Go ahead. I'm going to build it now. I have built you. I need to build you before I build the building." So that's what he did. He built us before he built the building.[45]

For many people, Evans embodied the best of the African American church's social activism. "To me, he epitomized strong leadership in the black community," Rush said. "I was fascinated with his decision, rather than cave in, to just let Fellowship remain half built. To me, that half-built church was a symbol to resoluteness, to honoring a higher power rather than the political might of a Daley or any other mayor."

Rev. Stephen Thurston was a teenager when Evans dared to defy Richard J. Daley and the Chicago political machine. Evans's decision to support King, Thurston said, influenced a new generation of leaders who would one day become ministers and advocates for marginalized communities in the spirit of Evans and King. "When we saw Reverend Evans standing up like that, as young fellows here in this city, it became for us a model to how we should respond to the social-justice issues in this country," Thurston said. "And we lined up behind him because he was that living mentor that we needed in that way."[46] Some believed Evans's leadership in welcoming King to Chicago was providential. "He came at a time when we really needed Rev. Clay Evans," former Illinois governor Pat Quinn said. "It was a tense and turbulent, controversial time where things had to be changed and reformed. The walls of discrimination had to come tumbling down, and he was our Joshua. He led us on that mission, and he spoke out, and the trumpets were heard. And those walls did come tumbling down, thanks to the leadership of Rev. Clay Evans and Fellowship Missionary Baptist Church."[47]

After King's assassination, Rev. Otis Moss Jr. shared a poignant moment with Evans while they marched together in King's funeral procession through Atlanta's streets. During the procession, Moss and Evans reminisced about their journey fighting for civil rights over the years. Moss had learned, through personal conversations with King, how much Evans had sacrificed on King's behalf in Chicago, and that through such sacrifices, Evans had become a mentor to someone as powerful and accomplished as Dr. King. Recalling all this in 2012, Moss said:

We walked together in 1968 from Ebenezer Baptist Church in the funeral procession to Morehouse College. I was carrying a wreath ahead of the mule-drawn wagon and casket of Dr. King, and Dr. Clay Evans was beside me and a part of that upfront contingent in front of the pallbearers who accompanied the wagon and the casket. This was perhaps a three- to five-mile walk. And we had a chance to converse on that journey. I also knew quite well through Dr. King and others the support that Rev. Evans had given to Dr. King in Chicago when doors had been closed in a most unwelcoming way. . . . Dr. King's journey, his work, his coming to Chicago—and this is following Selma—could not have been what it was without the leadership, on the ground, of Rev. Dr. Clay Evans. Dr. Evans really provided a home, a spiritual home, and literally a welcoming center for Dr. King.[48]

Father Pfleger recalled a conversation he once had with King's wife, Coretta Scott King, who described King's appreciation of the friendship Evans had extended to him in Chicago. "I remember Coretta King, you know, years and years later, telling me how Dr. King felt that . . . Pastor Evans, as a prominent pastor standing with him, made an unbelievable importance and impact in the city of Chicago. [Evans] received an awful lot of hate for it, but he was not willing to compromise."[49]

Historian Timuel Black confirmed King's intense appreciation for Evans's friendship and support. Evans had helped to bring together South and West Side ministers who supported King.[50] These coalitions of ministers were invaluable support systems for King in Chicago. "Dr. King knew and cherished Reverend Evans," Black said. Black praised Evans's courage for openly supporting Dr. King while in the midst of a construction project that required city leaders' endorsement. "There were those who wondered how in the world would he have the nerve to do that," Black said about Evans's defiance of city leaders during the turbulent years of the 1960s. The harsh anti-civil-rights climate swirling in Chicago at the time of Evans's stand with King and civil rights made him, Black said, "heroic to say the least."[51]

Evans's refusal to compromise his social-justice agenda was always motivated first and fundamentally by his conviction that as a pastor, he was called to intercede on behalf of others, especially those who were victims of injustice. Evans felt called in particular to African Americans being harassed by unjust systems in Chicago. "I tried to serve those people, not just preach to them. I believe you have to have a holistic ministry," Evans said. It was important to Evans to not confine religion to the four walls of the church. "I believe the salt ought to get in the community and get involved with social, civic, political things, because they help to make the community better. And if I'm salt, I have to help make the community better. . . . You find some means of meeting the needs. You just can't sit back."

Amazingly, amid all the hate and hostility, Fellowship's members did not abandon ship. "The Ship" stood by its captain. Even during the coldest, darkest, windiest hours, Fellowship's members offered whatever support was needed. "The Lord kept us together through all that shame, disgrace, and humiliation," Evans testified. "And that's amazing. Because usually in those situations, people leave you like rats leaving a sinking ship. But the Lord kept us strong." Even as the tempest was raging.

NOTES

1. Rev. Jesse Jackson Sr., interview by author, 2012, Fellowship Missionary Baptist Church, Chicago.

2. Dorothy June Rose, *From Plough Handle to Pulpit: The Life Story of Rev. Clay Evans, a Man with a Mission* (Warminster, PA: Neibauer, 1981), 43.

3. Fellowship Missionary Baptist Church, "Our History," http://fellowshipchicago.com/history/.

4. Rose, *From Plough Handle to Pulpit*, 44.

5. Rose, *From Plough Handle to Pulpit*, 44.

6. Taylor Branch, *At Canaan's Edge: America in the King Years, 1965–68* (New York: Simon & Schuster, 2007), 252.

7. Branch, *At Canaan's Edge*, 321.

8. Branch, *At Canaan's Edge*, 321.

9. Clayborne Carson, ed., *The Autobiography of Martin Luther King, Jr.* (New York: Warner, 1998), 298.

10. Carson, *The Autobiography of Martin Luther King, Jr.*, 298.

11. Carson, ed., *Autobiography of Martin Luther King, Jr.*, 298–99.

12. Rose, *From Plough Handle to Pulpit*, 45.

13. Rev. Jesse Jackson, interview by the author, 2012, Fellowship Missionary Baptist Church, Chicago.

14. Chuck Bowen, interview by author, Friday, February 8, 2013, Chicago.

15. Karen Hawkins, "King '66 Visit to Chicago Not a Warm

Welcome," *Chicago Defender*, January 18, 2011, http://tinyurl.com/
ydeghuuf.

16. Hawkins, "King '66 Visit to Chicago Not a Warm Welcome."

17. Don Terry, "Northern Exposure: Nothing He'd Seen in the South
    Prepared Martin Luther King for the Streets of Marquette Park in
    1966," *Chicago Tribune*, January 15, 2006, http://tinyurl.com/
    yc4loy9x.

18. Rev. Jesse Jackson, interview.

19. For scholarly treatment of back religious leaders in conflict, see
    Peter J. Paris, *Black Religious Leaders in Conflict* (Louisville:
    Westminster John Knox, 1991).

20. Taylor Branch, *Pillar of Fire: America in the King Years, 1963–65*
    (New York: Simon and Schuster, 1998), 24.

21. Chuck Bowen, interview by the author, 2013, Chicago.

22. Minister Louis Farrakhan, interview by the author, September 28,
    2012, Rev. Clay Evans's home, Chicago.

23. R. Drew Smith and Frederick C. Harris, eds., *Black Churches and
    Local Politics: Clergy Influence, Organizational Partnerships, and Civic
    Empowerment* (Lanham, MD: Rowman & Littlefield, 2005), 120.

24. Pervis Spann with Linda C. Walker, *The 40 Year Spann of WVON*
    (Chicago: National Academy of the Blues, 2003), 107–8.

25. Jennifer Searcy, "The Voice of the Negro: African American
    Radio, WVON, and the Struggle for Civil Rights in Chicago"
    (PhD diss., Loyola University, 2003), paper 688, p. 117,
    http://tinyurl.com/y7gpcxya.

26. Pat Quinn, interview by the author, 2012, James R. Thompson Center, Chicago.

27. Michael Pfleger, interview by the author, 2012, Saint Sabina Church, Chicago.

28. Rose, *From Plough Handle to Pulpit*, 45.

29. Travis J. Dempsey, *An Autobiography of Black Politics* (Chicago: Urban Research, 1987), 355.

30. Rose, *From Plough Handle to Pulpit*, 45.

31. Clay Evans quoted in Rose, *From Plough Handle to Pulpit*, 46.

32. Clay Evans quoted in Dempsey, *An Autobiography of Black Politics*, 354. Also see Manya A. Brachear, "Pastor Passes Torch of Gospel Choir," *Chicago Tribune*, May 30, 2010; Derrick Blakley, "Rev. Evans Hails Progress of PUSH," *Chicago Tribune*, July 7, 1974; Karen Hawkins, "King '66 Visit to Chicago Not a Warm Welcome."

33. Michael Pfleger, interview.

34. Richard M. Daley, interview by the author, June 1, 2012, James R. Thompson Center, Chicago.

35. Louis Farrakhan, interview.

36. Don Sharp, interview by the author, 2012, Faith Tabernacle Baptist Church, Chicago.

37. Rev. Dr. Otis Moss Jr., interview by Patty Nolan-Fitzgerald, Trinity United Church of Christ, Chicago.

38. Rose, *From Plough Handle to Pulpit*, 46.

39. Clay Evans quoted in Rose, *From Plough Handle to Pulpit*, 46–47.

40. Rose, *From Plough Handle to Pulpit*, 47.

41. Frederick C. Harris, "Black Churches and Machine Politics in Chicago," in Smith and Harris, *Black Churches and Local Politics*, 124.

42. Rose, *From Plough Handle to Pulpit*, 47.

43. Michael Pfleger, interview.

44. Bobby Rush, interview by the author, 2012, Chicago.

45. Lou Della Evans-Reid, interview by the author, 2012, Fellowship Missionary Baptist Church, Chicago.

46. Rev. Stephen Thurston, interview by the author, 2012, Fellowship Missionary Baptist Church, Chicago.

47. Pat Quinn, interview.

48. Rev. Dr. Otis Moss Jr., interview by Patty Nolan-Fitzgerald, 2012, Trinity United Church of Christ, Chicago.

49. Michael Pfleger, interview.

50. Timuel Black, interview by Patty Nolan-Fitzgerald, 2013, Chicago.

51. Timuel Black, interview by Patty Nolan-Fitzgerald.

14

BREAKING BREAD TOGETHER

I think that many of us really don't like to get involved, so we just keep our gospel between the stained-glass windows and painted walls.

—Rev. Clay Evans

THE EARLY 1990s—During Evans's pastoral ministry at Fellowship Missionary Baptist Church, he worked with many talented ministers. One such minister was Rev. Shelvin Jerome Hall. Hall began pastoring the Friendship Baptist Church, located on Chicago's West Side, in 1955. The church had been organized in 1897 and in the 1920s was recognized as one of the leading congregations on the West Side. By 1956, the church had become one of the city's most prominent Baptist churches. The church grew significantly under Hall's leadership. By the 1980s, the congregation had moved twice. Friendship Baptist boasted a variety of education, leadership, and youth programs. In 1990, Hall was elected president of the Baptist General State Convention and served two consecutive three-year terms until 1996. Hall was a powerful force on Chicago's West Side, and he wielded tremendous influence throughout Chicago.[1]

In those days, Hall and Friendship Church resembled Evans and Fellowship Church in many ways. Both pastors boasted congregations with mass choirs, large memberships, and an explicit commitment to social justice. But Hall, a West Side pastor, and Evans, a South Side pastor, often found themselves immersed in a strange, citywide rivalry between West and South Side clergy. Somehow, West Side churches had become associated with more emotional, folksy, and less scholarly styles of preaching, while South Side pastors were considered by many to be more intellectual and erudite scholar-preachers. Evans recalled this perception: "In Chicago, the West Side is the less progressive side. . . . They [West Side pastors] think that the South Side feels like they are better than they are." Evans admitted he used to tell a joke to other pastors that the social protocol on the South Side was for pastors to send any of their unruly, unrefined church members to the West Side. "We'll put them on the West until they become civilized," Evans said, laughing. While these perceptions were often approached with humor, Evans confessed these perceptions at times created serious barriers between South and West Side pastors. "There has always been a division, and I don't know why, between the South Side and the West Side. It's like two different cities," he said.

While the origins of these stereotypes are unknown, they were real and fueled intense competition. At times, tensions even erupted between Hall and Evans. They were two competent leaders negotiating Chicago's political machinery and social ills with confidence, drive, and immense talent. Their natural competitiveness ignited sparks that at times converged into fire. The two pastors would challenge each other publicly, sometimes humorously and sometimes heatedly. It was well known that Hall and Evans jousted verbally from time to time. Still, there was always respect between them. Chuck Bowen, who worked with both pastors as a former aide to Mayor Richard M. Daley, remembered a grand gesture of respect Evans extended to Hall during Hall's funeral. "When Shelvin died," Bowen recalled, "Clay walked into the church and was not on the program, but after he finished [addressing the congregation], the guy who was supposed to give the eulogy said, 'I'm not about to give the eulogy after this.' Reverend Evans really preached a fantastic sermon. Of course, he had a lot of material on Shelvin," Bowen said jokingly.

In general, there were few instances of serious, sustained collaboration between West and South Side ministers on social issues that affected their communities. In black communities in the city, hardworking residents paid higher rent than their white counterparts living in the city's more affluent North Side. Often, the only affordable housing available for African Americans on the South and West Sides was located in slum-riddled neighborhoods or housing projects. Moreover, African Americans were denied jobs from the very local companies that made products they purchased. These conditions created in Chicago what prominent sociologist and economist William Julius Wilson called a black urban underclass.[2]

Indeed, great strides in social and economic justice had been made since the northern campaign for civil rights in the mid-1960s. But by the early 1990s, Chicago's South and West Sides were plagued by gang violence, rampant poverty, and the many city leaders who failed to take seriously the plights of poor and lower-middle-class African Americans. Regrettably, the negative perceptions that South and West Side black pastors held about one another often prevented any serious or sustained collaboration. Thus, many of the problems affecting black communities went unaddressed by black clergy in any collective manner. It would take a table and a meal to end the standoff.

Richard M. Daley, whose father, former mayor Richard J. Daley, had opposed Evans's support of King three decades earlier, was elected mayor of Chicago in 1989. Evans, then sixty-four years old, had great hopes for Chicago's new mayor. The younger Daley's election provided a unique occasion for South and West Side pastors to unite in a common cause to improve the lives of African Americans in the city. Following Daley's election, the administration acknowledged city leaders' fractured relationship with the black community in general and black pastors in particular. Some black political leaders saw the opportunity to utilize Daley's influence to mend these relationships. Chuck Bowen was one of these leaders. Bowen was serving as a county commissioner when Daley began his campaign for mayor. Bowen's years and experience in that position had earned him the respect and trust of many of Chicago's elected leaders, including Daley. If elected, Daley promised, he would offer Bowen a position in his administration. After Daley's election, Bowen approached Daley with a request to be appointed as a liaison between city leaders and the city's black clergy.

Bowen told Evans about his proposal to Daley. Evans eventually approached Daley and expressed his desire to see Bowen appointed to serve as the bridge connecting black clergy and the communities they served with Chicago's politicians. Daley agreed. Bowen's primary responsibility was to establish a more direct, collaborative relationship between the city's black religious leaders and the Daley administration. Daley, Bowen, and Evans would soon realize how important this partnership was in mending already-tense relationships between African Americans and city leaders.

During the first year of Daley's mayoral term, a bitter disagreement erupted between Daley's administration and black clergy when a tight city budget threatened to end the annual Dr. Martin Luther King Jr. breakfast celebration. It had become a tradition for the mayor's office to host an annual breakfast in honor of the national holiday celebrating the civil rights leader. Eugene Sawyer, Chicago's second African American mayor, had started the tradition during his term from 1987 to 1989. By the time Daley was elected mayor, the annual King Day Breakfast had become a welcomed tradition. It was a time of breaking bread and fellowship, reflecting on the significant gains in civil rights, and looking optimistically toward the collaborative partnerships between clergy and politicians to secure future progress in the city. Bowen approached Kathy Osterman, then director of the Mayor's Office of Special Events, to discuss details surrounding plans for the annual King Breakfast. Osterman informed Bowen there was not enough money in the city's budget to continue the tradition. Bowen immediately objected and emphatically voiced his dismay to Daley. "I told him . . . this is a mistake if you don't have the King Day Breakfast. Mayor Sawyer started it. You should definitely do it!"[3] Hoping to resolve the issue before tensions caused further damage to the already-fractured relationship between black clergy and city leaders, Daley asked Bowen to organize local black ministers to find a creative solution. Bowen turned to Evans. Evans began urging black pastors to unite under the common cause of King's legacy. Shelvin Hall also urged black pastors to become involved in saving the annual breakfast. According to Bowen, Hall even opened the doors of his church for meetings and strategy sessions. "When we started to organize, it was Shelvin Hall's church that we first took the ministers," said Bowen. Under Evans and Hall's organizing efforts, ministers from both the South and West Sides formed a coalition to save the annual King Day Breakfast by financing it with their own money.

Since the entire event was now being funded by a coalition of the city's black religious leaders, the mayor's office had no choice but to collaborate with black clergy and hold the annual King Day Breakfast. The coalition of ministers negotiated with Daley's administration to hold the event at the Hyatt Hotel's Grand Ballroom. On the day of the event, Bowen said, some city leaders were skeptical the event would yield a large enough turnout to justify the time and energy spent planning it. "Nobody thought that it was really going to succeed that year," Bowen said, referring to some of the city's leaders. The city's event planners, Bowen added, had only requested use of a small part of the Grand Ballroom for the event. Bowen boasted, "They had one little section, and that's where the breakfast was going to be. But that morning, they had to keep opening sections up. . . . It was so full that people were standing!"

Ironically, the first major initiative of this coalition of African American ministers from the city's South and West Sides was to rescue an event honoring a man whose presence in Chicago had once bitterly divided them. Energized by the success of their inaugural venture, the coalition of South and West Side black clergy began discussing the more pressing social issues its members might confront. The King Day Breakfast was an important symbolic rallying point from which the city's black clergy could embark on a mission to address the larger problems plaguing their communities. Evans and members of the clergy coalition discerned a unique opportunity to improve the quality of life for black Chicagoans and to work to build a better Chicago. The members of this new coalition decided to call themselves the Concerned Clergy for a Better Chicago.

After the creation of the Concerned Clergy for a Better

Chicago, black pastors in Chicago had a significant platform from which they could quickly access city leaders and initiate serious conversations about various injustices throughout the city. For Evans, this coalition of black pastors was a manifestation of the hopes many African Americans had fought for during the turbulent years of the 1960s. By speaking through the members of the Concerned Clergy for a Better Chicago, African Americans in Chicago had a much louder voice to reach the ears of Chicago's most powerful decision makers. The Concerned Clergy for a Better Chicago took up one cause after the next, trumpeting unapologetically that the health, well-being, and dignity of black Chicagoans mattered and should be secured whenever threatened. With great momentum, passion, and closer proximity to Chicago's power brokers, the Concerned Clergy for a Better Chicago swept through the city!

NOTES

1. Friendship Baptist Church, "History of Friendship Baptist Church," http://www.fbcchicago.org/history.html.

2. See William Julius Wilson, *When Work Disappears* (New York: Vintage, 1997); Wilson, *The Declining Significance of Race* (Chicago: University of Chicago Press, 2012).

3. Chuck Bowen, interview by the author, Friday, February 8, 2013, Chicago.

15

SWEEPING
THROUGH THE CITY

BETWEEN THE EARLY AND LATE 1990s—By the early 1990s, many African American pastors in Chicago had become highly suspicious of elected leaders and frustrated with the inner workings of the city's political process. Many believed city leaders had largely neglected a host of serious social problems in black communities. Many blacks in Chicago continued to live in slum-like public housing. Gang violence continued to erupt on city streets. Menacing potholes went unattended. Police officers engaged in racial profiling. And there was an underrepresentation of black leadership within city government. These were just a few of the problems black Chicagoans faced at the beginning of Richard M. Daley's first mayoral term. Three decades after Martin Luther King Jr.'s campaign in Chicago, many of the city's black residents had become less optimistic that brokering relationships with the city's elected leaders would help address their concerns. However, Clay Evans and members of the Concerned Clergy for a Better Chicago believed collaboration with city leaders was necessary.

Many of the challenges facing black communities in Chicago in the early 1990s remained unaddressed because there was not a viable platform from which black residents could articulate their concerns to the city's power brokers. Evans and Bowen recognized the need for a communicative and relational bridge between city leaders and black communities in Chicago. They devised a strategy to help address various social problems in Chicago while helping city leaders to understand the needs of black citizens. The Concerned Clergy for a Better Chicago proposed a plan to assign to each major city department a minister who would serve as a liaison between the city and black residents. Evans and Bowen believed having a minister as a liaison in each city department would help mitigate concerns that city leaders were unconcerned about and disconnected from issues shaping black life in Chicago. According to the clergy coalition's proposed plan, major city departments such as police, fire, housing, and streets and sanitation would begin interfacing with at least one black clergyperson. City department directors would then bring community concerns with their departments to their assigned minister liaison. The clergy liaisons would then serve as a bridge between city leaders and black residents. "Reverend Evans and I talked about it. You have so many things that happen that you're not on top of in Chicago," Bowen said, referring to the host of unaddressed social concerns African Americans faced at the time. "This was a way to get on top of these issues."[1]

Mayor Daley agreed to the plan, and city leaders voted to adopt the new initiative. The process for selecting clergy liaisons was simple. Bowen would recommend potential candidates to Evans. Then Bowen and Evans would discuss the merits of each candidate for the role. Sometimes they disagreed. But ultimately, Bowen said, it was Evans who determined which candidate Bowen recommended to Mayor Daley. Then city council members appointed each clergy liaison as an official clergy commissioner. To ensure fair representation, the process involved alternating appointments between South and West Side ministers.

These clergy commissioners served on most of the city's departments. Thus, the new initiative gave black Chicagoans and black clergy an unprecedented platform to influence city policies and procedures. These ministers were not few in number. And while the clergy commissioners served alongside city leaders, Bowen explained, they were adamant about maintaining autonomy in determining their agenda. "The hardest part of the job was always trying to get the political establishment to understand that the church was in the lead of this thing," Bowen recalled. "Because there are more preachers talking to people on eleven o'clock a.m. on Sunday than any politician can get."

Evans would hold regular meetings of the Concerned Clergy for a Better Chicago, to which Mayor Daley would be invited to speak. During these meetings, members of the clergy coalition provided Daley with an agenda of what they wanted him to address with city leaders. Never had there been such an intentional and collaborative relationship between Chicago's black pastors and politicians, Bowen claimed. However, the strength of these relationships between the black clergy, their communities, and city leaders would soon be tested.

The clergy liaison initiative gained momentum quickly. Many needs within black communities were heard and addressed. However, one persistent problem continued to menace black communities: violence. As President Ronald Reagan's war on drugs escalated, so did Chicago's street violence. Ironically, the social ills that Martin Luther King Jr. and the SCLC had attempted to address in Chicago in the mid-1960s had intensified by the 1990s. Tragically, King's prediction had become a reality: the unaddressed chronic poverty in certain black communities in Chicago was exploding in the form of violence. Evans and other leaders of the Concerned Clergy for a Better Chicago began conversations with city leaders to devise potential solutions to the city's growing problem of violence. There was a strong belief among black pastors that the city's police department could and should play a key role in turning the tide of Chicago's violence. Almost immediately, black clergy began lobbying city leaders to consider hiring a black police superintendent. The logic behind the idea was straightforward. A black police superintendent would bring to the city's police force a perspective about the particular issues in Chicago's black communities. Just as the appointed clergy commissioners ensured that the black community's concerns were more adequately addressed, many black clergy believed, a black police superintendent would ensure that adequate

attention was given to the complex social realities con-
tributing to violence in black communities.

Evans made sure that hiring a black police superintendent was a top priority for the Concerned Clergy for a Better Chicago. A consensus quickly formed. Having secured
the support of black pastors on the South and West Sides,
Evans began meeting with certain city leaders privately,
beginning with Mayor Daley. Evans came to these meetings
with a single agenda: to pressure the mayor to hire a black
police superintendent. He was bold and unapologetic.
Eventually, Evans claimed, with enough prodding from
himself and other black clergy, Daley consented. Evans
interpreted Daley's consent as assurance that the city would
hire a black superintendent. Then sixty-eight years old,
Evans felt his optimism about the democratic process and
Chicago politics to be at an all-time high. The clergy coalition was fulfilling its purpose. There was no denying the
coalition's success in brokering relationships with city leaders to improve the quality of life in Chicago's black communities. The hiring of a black police superintendent would
be a major victory for the Concerned Clergy for a Better
Chicago and would demonstrate that structural change in
Chicago was occurring.

As far as Evans was concerned, he and Mayor Daley had
a gentlemen's agreement that an African American would
be hired as the new police superintendent. But negotiations
soon soured. Bowen remembered the exact moment when
things fell apart. During a visit to one of the city's Hispanic
communities, Daley met significant opposition. Hispanic

residents, also concerned about the violence occurring in their communities, pressed Daley to hire a Hispanic police superintendent. "He went to the Hispanic community, and he got beat up pretty bad," Bowen said about the community's criticism of Daley. "So he caved." When time came to appoint the city's next police superintendent, Daley hired, Matt L. Rodriguez, the city's first Hispanic police superintendent.[2] Like Evans, Bowen also believed from meetings with Daley that Chicago's next police superintendent would be an African American. "The mayor said he was going to hire a black superintendent but did not," Bowen said.

Bowen knew and rightly feared that any fallout between Evans and Daley could damage the relationship between Daley's administration and the clergy coalition permanently. "This was early in the Daley administration, and the clergy coalition was still young," Bowen worried. Bowen knew Evans would be angry. He rushed to meet with Evans to calm any intense emotions before Evans confronted Daley in person. Too much was at stake to risk tearing apart the clergy coalition. Bowen reassured Evans that he had no intention of letting Daley off the hook for breaking what Bowen and Evans believed was a gentlemen's agreement. Bowen remembered saying to Evans, "Let's go give him hell," referring to Daley. However, Bowen convinced Evans they needed to be strategic and tactful. Now that the damage had been done, the two leaders would approach Daley with an attitude that Daley owed them. Since many African Americans had trusted the clergy coalition to negotiate the hiring of a black police superintendent, Evans and Bowen felt Daley owed them for what both felt was a broken promise.

Shortly after Daley hired Matt L. Rodriguez as Chicago's new police superintendent, Evans and Bowen met privately with Daley. The three leaders met briefly at McCormick Place Convention Center, where Daley was scheduled to speak for an event. Upon Daley's arrival, Bowen, Evans, and Daley's assistant found an empty room in which to talk. Just as soon as the door closed behind them, Evans let the mayor have it. "He said, 'God damn it, you lied to me!'" Bowen recalled later. Immediately, Daley's assistant tried to calm Evans down. But Evans, overwhelmed with emotion, turned his anger on Daley's assistant. According to Bowen, Evans turned to Daley's assistant and said, "Don't you ever in your life get in between me and this man [Daley]. You shut up and don't say a word to me!" The room fell silent. "My heart was in my hand," Bowen recalled. The meeting ended without any resolution. But both Evans and Daley agreed to meet again soon.

Over the next few weeks, Bowen and Evans agreed that the way forward was to approach the negotiation table with the perspective that Daley had broken a promise. Framing their grievance in terms of a broken promise, the two concluded, would be a more persuasive argument than spewing the anger both felt. In their meetings with Daley, Evans and Bowen shifted the conversation from betrayal to atonement. The tactic worked. From that point on, Bowen claimed, Daley's administration was accommodating to the clergy commission's proposals. "The truth is that every-thing kind of flowed for us after that," Bowen recalled.

The tensions between Evans and Daley eventually sub-sided. Despite the brief strain in their relationship, both men agreed that they stood a better chance of meeting the needs of Chicago's most vulnerable citizens if they worked together. Over the next five years, Evans and Daley devel-oped a highly productive partnership as the black-clergy coalition continued to work alongside city leaders. To be sure, Evans and Daley had disagreements. However, the mutual respect both had for one another kept both men returning to the negotiation table, always motivated by the prospect of improving the lives of Chicagoans. During the five years following Evans and Daley's brief fallout over the police superintendent hire, the Concerned Clergy for a Bet-ter Chicago and city leaders enjoyed a fruitful partnership. Roads were repaired. Poor sanitation in certain neighbor-hoods was improved. Complaints about housing conditions were addressed more swiftly. Instances of violence were approached more critically.

In 1996, Evans and Daley would collaborate again on a major initiative through the Concerned Clergy for a Better Chicago that strengthened the bond between the two men: renaming a stretch of highway after the late Bishop Henry Louis Ford. Bishop Ford's ministry was well known throughout Chicago and preceded Evans's own ministry by fifteen years. Ford had begun preaching in Lexington, Mis-sissippi, in the 1930s and then moved to Chicago in 1933, when Evans was just eight years old. Ford organized Saint

Paul Church of God in Christ in 1935 and was elected bishop of Illinois in 1954 (four years after Evans founded Fellowship). In 1990, he was elected presiding bishop of the 8.5-million–member Church of God in Christ (COGIC).[3] Ford was an unwavering advocate of Evans during the civil rights movement. In fact, Ford was one of a few black pastors who had stood with Evans when many black ministers alienated Evans for supporting King. Ford's church, like Fellowship, celebrated the critical link between faith and social justice. He, too, believed in the importance of believers boldly incarnating the principles of their faith in their daily lives.

When Ford died in 1995, thousands attended his funeral. The large attendance signified the importance of his ministry to his members and to the city of Chicago. About a year after Ford's death, his son, Charles Ford, who succeeded his father as pastor of Saint Paul Church of God in Christ, called Bowen with a request to rename a stretch of highway in honor of his father. Given his father's prominence and accomplishments, Daley's administration received Ford's request warmly. The legacy of Ford's ministry was certainly strong enough to warrant such an honor. However, Bowen was informed there were some requirements that had to be met before the Daley administration could agree officially to approve Charles Ford's request. In particular, there had to be a demonstration to city leaders that the desire for Bishop Ford Expressway was a majority sentiment among Chicago's black community. In other words, there had to be proof that the sentiment to honor Bishop Ford existed beyond Ford's following within the

COGIC denomination. Again, Bowen immediately sought Evans's counsel. The two agreed the Concerned Clergy for a Better Chicago would be the ideal platform to demonstrate that wide support existed for renaming a highway after the late Bishop Ford.

Then seventy years old and a forty-five-year veteran Baptist pastor, Evans was well connected with Baptist circles in Chicago. But it would take more than support from Baptists in Chicago to move forward. Convincing city leaders to name a highway after Bishop Ford would require the Concerned Clergy for a Better Chicago to recruit significant interdenominational support. The task was daunting. However, the clergy coalition devised a clever strategy. Instead of approaching individual pastors in various denominations, they would approach conference presidents and bishops. Since these leaders presided over entire churches and denominations, it would be a more efficient use of time to convince these leaders to encourage their members to support the Bishop Ford Expressway initiative.

In addition to working with top denominational leaders, the clergy coalition secured support from several prominent city leaders who also felt strongly that Bishop Ford should be honored. These leaders flexed their influence at the top of the city's political machine. For instance, Evans pushed Ed Vrdolyak, who had served as an alderman, to reach out to then-governor Jim Edgar for support.[4] With the support of enough city leaders and black Chicagoans, the Concerned Clergy of Chicago demonstrated there was widespread support to name a highway after the late Bishop

Ford. After about six months, the city voted officially to change the name of the Calumet Expressway to the Bishop Ford Expressway. The victory was another testimony of the importance of Evans's leadership within the Concerned Clergy for a Better Chicago and within Chicago politics. The leadership Evans wielded as one of the clergy coalition's chief elders brokered unprecedented relationships among city leaders, black pastors, and black Chicagoans.

Unfortunately, the coalition dissipated after Evans retired from Fellowship in 2000. But during the height of its activity between 1990 and 2000, the Concerned Clergy for a Better Chicago served as a critical link between City Hall and the black community. The organization was instrumental in celebrating and protecting the dignity of black lives. The coalition's work with Richard M. Daley's administration demonstrates that Evans's principles were bigger than his politics. Clay Evans proved himself to be a bridge builder whose work with Daley's administration afforded the younger Daley opportunities to redefine his family legacy.

Under Evans's leadership, the Concerned Clergy for a Better Chicago is believed to have been the largest network of black clergy ever assembled in Chicago to work alongside of city leaders. While at the helm of Fellowship and the Concerned Clergy for a Better Chicago, Rev. Clay Evans sailed successfully through the treacherous waters of Chicago's social ills. He broke through the ice-blocked channels of Chicago's political machinery. Such organizational leadership, Evans said, is needed desperately in cities like Chicago today. Without an organization like the Concerned Clergy for a Better Chicago, Evans said, the city now misses critical opportunities to address community concerns directly, swiftly, and efficiently. With bold determination, Evans and the black-clergy coalition swept through the city, advocating for Chicago's most vulnerable citizens. Similar boldness and determination are needed today in cities like Chicago, Evans said, if the dignity of black lives and all lives is to be celebrated and protected.

NOTES

1. Chuck Bowen, interview by the author, Friday, February 8, 2013, Chicago.

2. Chicago Police Department, "History," http://tinyurl.com/y9ubc8mb.

3. "Bishop Louis Henry Ford; Head of Church of God in Christ," *Los Angeles Times*, April 2, 1995, http://tinyurl.com/y8y7r8h3.

4. Chuck Bowen, interview by the author, Friday, February 8, 2013, Chicago.

PART IV

DOCKING THE SHIP

16

THE CAPTAIN
RETIRES

THE LATE 1990s—One morning Evans awoke at 4:30 a.m., as he always did on Sunday mornings. He crawled out of bed, slowly. It was time to begin his many rituals to prepare for worship at Fellowship. Waking at such an early hour was normal for Evans. As a sharecropper in Brownsville, he had often been up before the sun broke the horizon and accomplished more by breakfast than most accomplished in an entire day. Early mornings were as normal for Evans as breathing.

Almost fifty years had passed since Evans had launched Fellowship's first worship service in September 1950 in that small chapel at A. R. Leak Funeral Home. Much had happened since then. Many of the beloved saints present at Fellowship's beginning had gone from the world. The precious infants Evans had blessed and children he had baptized were now adults with their own children. Decades had passed since Evans had ordained Rev. Consuella York, stood with Rev. Dr. Martin Luther King Jr., and fought for civil rights while sailing through Chicago's raging social and political tempests. After almost five decades in ministry, Evans had oceans of memories.

When Evans arrived at Fellowship that morning, he made his way to his office. His list of duties each Sunday was long: check phone messages, visit the Sunday school classes, give marching orders to the deacons, check in with the associate ministers, check in with the church staff, greet the children during children's church, sing at least one song during worship, preach the sermon, greet church members and visitors after worship, offer counseling to members in crisis, visit the sick and shut-in at their homes, visit those in the hospital. It all had begun to feel a little overwhelming. Evans's responsibilities on Sunday mornings started to feel almost too much to handle. After his many years in ministry, Evans began to feel the burden of aging.

As a twenty-five-year-old back in 1950, Evans had had endless energy reserves. As a young pastor, he had completed the host of pre-worship and post-worship rituals with vigor left to spare. But now, approaching his mid-seventies, Evans felt his body weakening. He hurt in places that didn't hurt before. He struggled to stand for long periods of time. His eyesight was worsening. His voice was growing softer. His aging body caused him to make mistakes. He began forgetting about appointments. He dismissed some problems because he didn't have the energy to deal with them. Not only was his body weakening, but Evans also began to lose the mental sharpness he needed to pastor effectively. As an older man, he could no longer fulfill his duties as pastor of "The Ship" with the intensity he once had. He could no longer press through the long hours, the late nights, and the early mornings. "I didn't have the strength, the energy, the mental alertness to deal with those kind of responsibilities," Evans explained. "I was losing some control. If you are losing control of a situation or yourself, you have to take the next step. Because otherwise it will destroy you."

Evans had to admit a difficult truth: it was time for him to step down as senior pastor of his beloved Fellowship Missionary Baptist Church. "Pastoring is 24/7. I loved it! There is just a lot involved in being a *real* pastor. That's what I wanted to be, and when I felt like I couldn't be that anymore, I decided it was time to retire as pastor." One of Evans's greatest fears as an aging pastor was that he would become a burden to his members. Evans had witnessed other pastors, close confidants, who were weary and worn from decades of faithful ministry. These pastors, Evans recalled, had begun to pester their members, nagging them, complaining to and about them, and even resenting them. These pastors had not lost love for their members. Rather, their brash behavior toward members was rooted in their refusal to acknowledge the grief they felt about the limitations their aging had imposed on their ministries. These pastors, Evans said, projected their own conscious and subconscious sorrows and exhaustions onto their members. "I didn't want to get to pestering people instead of pastoring people. And real Christians want a pastor," Evans said.

Rev. Dr. Jeremiah A. Wright, former pastor of President Barack Obama, remembered Evans expressing a similar philosophy to him when Wright was retiring as senior pastor of Trinity United Church of Christ in Chicago. "When I was retiring, he came to church one Sunday morning," Wright recalled. "He said, 'Is this true what I hear?' I had announced I was retiring. I said, 'It's not a rumor. It's fact. I'm going.' He said, 'Good, because after a while, you stop being a pastor, and you go to pestering.'"[1] Evans was determined to not pastor past his prime. He had witnessed too many aging pastor friends struggle to show their members the tenderness they had once offered effortlessly during their early years. "The older you get, you don't have the mental alertness, the physical strength, the patience to deal with church members," Evans said. "You have to have patience to deal with some members. So you want to be equipped to do a good job."

Painful images of colleagues who continued to pastor after age had diminished their ability to lead served as Evans's primary motivation to retire. "They're weakened. They can't preach. They don't have the patience to preach. And that memory goes bad." The consequences of refusing to admit such limitations, Evans said, are serious. "So, as you weaken, also your congregation weakens. You can't help them. They're trying to help you. They just feel sorry for you sitting up there. Their hearts go out for you. They ought to always have concern for you. But you want to be able to help them." Evans knew if he continued pastoring Fellowship, he would jeopardize the strength and vitality of the ministry he had worked so hard to build. In a May 30, 2010, *Chicago Tribune* article, Manya A. Brachear shed further light on Evans's reasoning for retiring from pastoral ministry a decade before most of his colleagues would turn over the reins of their churches. Brachear wrote, "Evans recognized that many pastors were staying past their prime and tarnishing their legacies by doing so. He didn't want to take away from any of the good he might have created."[2] Evans had to be honest with himself about what was happening to his body: "You lose some of your vitality, energy, and vision." He vowed to not be one of those pastors who refused to accept that their time to step down had come. "I had seen them standing in the pulpit, and they can't control their water," Evans said, referring to aging pastors he had known who lost control of their bodily functions and urinated on themselves in the pulpit. "The older they get, the weaker the church is. I didn't want to get to that point. I wanted to move on out of the way and let the church go on."

It was a painful truth, but Evans knew it was time to retire. "I wanted to be able to turn it loose. My friends asked, 'How can you turn something loose that you started?' It's not easy," Evans said frankly. But Evans knew it was the best thing for the church. "It's hard to walk away from something you give birth to. I could feel it in my spirit that I was going down. You need to give it up while you're still up, while you're still in the good favor of the people." Evans decided he would retire from Fellowship when he turned seventy-five. "I don't know where I got that from. I learned that some denominations retired their priests or preachers at seventy-five. I had been thinking about that," he explained.

After resolving to retire, Evans turned his attention to the business of naming his successor. "I was most interested in my legacy and the right person that could take it on from there and do great things for Fellowship, possibly things I hadn't thought of or couldn't do. Because life must go on." For Evans, it was critical that Fellowship's proud legacy continue. "If what you had in mind ended when you resigned, it wasn't much of a life to begin with," Evans resolved. It was crucial that he find the right person to succeed him. Of course, many ministers wanted Evans's job. The line to assume the helm of "The Ship" was long. "I was a little bit worried, because most of the young fellows I had come across were alcoholics, money chasers, and women chasers," Evans said. The pool of potential candidates was deep. But Evans was in search of the right candidate.

Complicating matters was the fact that Evans had about twelve associate ministers serving under him at Fellowship when he announced he would be retiring. Some were hopeful Evans might name them as his successor. However, Evans communicated to each of his associate ministers individually that Fellowship's new pastor would not be selected from ministers serving at Fellowship. That decision angered some who felt they had served faithfully long enough to deserve the assignment. "They didn't like it too much," Evans recalled. Time was also a factor. Evans knew it was possible he could die before appointing his successor. In anticipation of such an event, Evans left Fellowship's leaders with a list of the qualities he wanted in the church's next senior pastor. Education was at the very top of his wish list. Evans wanted his successor to be a young man with at least a bachelor's degree. "Now here I am with no degree, but I emphasized that he must have a degree," Evans insisted. Further, his successor had to have a strong commitment to youth. Evans continued, "I've always had a strong educational program for my children."

Interestingly, Evans found his successor in the most unexpected way. About the time he began searching for a successor, a young preacher named Charles Jenkins had begun his ministry in Chicago. Jenkins had attended Moody Bible Institute and earned a bachelor of science degree in Christian education. He was also a student at Trinity Evangelical Seminary. Jenkins, in his early twenties at the time, was preaching regularly in different churches throughout Chicago. He was gaining a reputation as a dynamic, charismatic preacher. Jenkins, like most ministers in Chicago, knew of Evans's ministry and was aware of Fellowship's proud history. There were many ministry opportunities for a young preacher like Jenkins. But Jenkins felt that God had called him to one particular ministry: Fellowship. "I like to call it a God story," Jenkins said. "The Lord had placed this idea on my heart that I would lead Fellowship. I had never met Reverend Evans. I had never been to Fellowship. I grew up in another denominational framework, a Holiness church. So I didn't know much about the Baptist Church at all. And I told . . . one of my best friends, who happened to pastor a church, who told me I was crazy—out of my mind!"

Evans and Jenkins first met at a meeting of local clergy at Fellowship. "It just so happened that Rev. Charles Jenkins came along," Evans said. "It was a peculiar thing how we met. I can't explain it." Evans had established an organization called the African American Religious Connection (AARC), which convened ministers about using media, such as radio, television broadcasting, and gospel music to have an impact on the surrounding culture. AARC had a youth division that was in need of expansion. Rev. Janette Wilson, one of Evans's team leaders at AARC at the time, had heard about Jenkins's reputation as a charismatic preacher. Wilson asked Jenkins if he was interested in helping expand AARC's youth division. "I said, 'I'd be happy to,'" Jenkins recalled. "I put together an eight- to ten-page proposal, and my wife, who was my girlfriend then, printed it up, and I called Janette and said, 'I got a proposal.'" Wilson then told Jenkins to come by Fellowship one Thursday to drop off his proposal. "She said, 'I will look at it and see if I can use anything out of it. And we'll go forward.' So I showed up that Thursday in my Martin Luther King garb—black suit, black tie, black hard-bottom shoes—and I asked for Janette Wilson."

What followed, Jenkins described, was both humorous and fortuitous:

They said, "We'll get her for you. Go downstairs in our fellowship hall, and wait there, and we'll have her come over." Janette never came. A gentleman came over and said, "Are you Charles Jenkins?" I said, "I am." And he said, "Is that your proposal?" I said, "It is." He said, "I'm supposed to take it and make about thirty or forty copies of it for the meeting today." I said, "Sir, nobody's supposed to see this. Janette told me to drop it off. I'm going back to school. She's going to call me and let me know whether she can use it." I'm scared to death. I said to him, "I'm supposed to drop this off and go back to school."

He said, "Sir, if you don't hand me that proposal, Reverend Evans is going to be very upset with you." I said, "How is he going to be upset with me? He doesn't even know me." So he pulls out this clipboard and says, "Sir, do you see your name is on this list to present today? If you don't hand me that proposal, Reverend Evans, when he gets to your name, he's going to say some very unkind things about you for not showing at his meeting."

So I reluctantly hand over the proposal, and I ended up at this meeting I wasn't supposed to be at. Reverend Evans gets to me. He stands up and says, "Rev. Charles Jenkins. Rev. Charles Jenkins, please rise." So I stand, and my knees are knocking under the table. I started speaking, and in Reverend Evans's own words, at the moment I began to speak, God yelled in his ear, "That's your successor!" And that's how I got here.[3]

Evans recalled the story vividly. "I had never met him," Evans explained. "My spirit agreed with him. And I made that prediction the first time I heard him." After Jenkins's presentation, Evans approached him, and the two met for the first time. He told Jenkins that he wanted to appoint him as Fellowship's next senior pastor. Referring to Jenkins, Evans said, "He was surprised I asked him, because I didn't know him." After that day, Evans took Jenkins under his wing.

During the next two years, Evans groomed Jenkins to take over the reins at Fellowship. For Evans, the two-year transition period was critical. He wanted to make sure Jenkins had the integrity necessary to serve as Fellowship's pastor. "So he hung around me for a couple of years before it became official. I was more concerned about his character," Evans admitted. The process Evans utilized to select Jenkins as the new pastor was autocratic. "I just kind of appointed him. There really wasn't a vote for him. When you've stayed with a group as long as I have and you have not betrayed them, they accept your judgment. They have confidence in you because they have seen your character." However, not everyone shared Evans's enthusiasm over the process he used to select Jenkins. In fact, some of the church staff urged Evans to reconsider. "They said to me, 'Reverend, don't be so emotional. You don't even know him!'" But Evans was convinced he had heard from the Holy Spirit.

The two-year transition period was a time for Evans to mentor Jenkins. Jenkins attended service each Sunday. For the most part, Jenkins was received well by the congregation. But his presence understandably caused tensions with some of the church staff and members. After all, Jenkins's attendance at Fellowship was indisputable evidence to Fellowship's members that their beloved pastor of almost fifty years was indeed retiring. Everyone knew Evans would eventually retire. Up to this point, however, all talk of Evans's retirement was abstract. But seeing Jenkins in worship every Sunday meant Evans's retirement was happening.

After getting through their initial stages of grief, Fellowship's members began making plans for an epic farewell to celebrate Evans's half century as Fellowship's pastor. That day came on Sunday, December 10, 2000, exactly fifty years after Evans launched Fellowship. It was a memorable celebration.

Evans promised Jenkins the same freedom to shepherd Fellowship that he had enjoyed. He vowed to Jenkins that he would not interfere and that he would not visit or worship at Fellowship often. "Very seldom I go there," Evans said, explaining, "so they can focus on him." Evans was determined to "back off" and let Jenkins have "full rein." But he made sure to stay "close enough that if he needs me, I can help." The formula has worked well for Evans and Jenkins. Jenkins understood and respected the special relationship older members of Fellowship shared with Evans. Further, Jenkins understood the value of supporting moments of pastoral care that required Evans's presence. "I do quite a few funerals of the old members, because they know me and I know them," Evans said. Evans described his relationship with Jenkins as one of mutual respect. "He's good to me. I try to be good to him. And the members know that. They don't come running to me, saying, 'Reverend Jenkins is doing this.'"

This loving relationship between a new pastor and his veteran predecessor doesn't always develop. Often, pastoral predecessors fail to let go of the reins fully. Instead, they interfere with their successor's work, sometimes secretly, sometimes not. "I ain't got no business making a decision," Evans said, explaining his understanding of his role as pastor emeritus of Fellowship. "I think if this kind of thing was really understood and carried out with other churches, that pastors would get along better with their successors."

Evans is proud of the leadership Jenkins has offered since becoming Fellowship's senior pastor in 2000. "So far, he hasn't disappointed me. He's done an excellent job. . . . The church is just growing. He's doing an excellent job," Evans said excitedly. Similarly, Jenkins expressed his pride in Evans and all that his ministry has offered Fellowship, the city of Chicago, and beyond. "He is iconic," Jenkins said. "He is a father, a mentor, adviser, pioneer, innovator. I mean, I could keep going on and on. There are not enough words in the dictionary to describe him. He's a hero and a trailblazer."[4]

After retiring as captain of "The Ship," Evans finally got to relax from the rigors of full-time pastoral ministry. He had big plans for retirement. He would spend more time with family. He would travel more. He would preach when he felt able and led. Evans had a lot planned for his season of retirement. Little did Evans know, his plans were about to be postponed. A serious illness festered silently within him. In April 2001, just four months after retiring from Fellowship, doctors told Rev. Clay Evans terrifying news: he had just six months to live.

NOTES

1. Rev. Jeremiah A. Wright, interview by the author, 2013, Dallas.

2. Manya A. Brachear, "Pastor Passes Torch of Gospel Choir," *Chicago Tribune*, May 30, 2010, http://tinyurl.com/y86fmjgh.

3. Rev. Charles Jenkins, interview by the author, 2012, Fellowship Missionary Baptist Church, Chicago.

4. Rev. Charles Jenkins, interview.

17

I'VE GOT A TESTIMONY

God let me get up out of that bed at Rush Hospital to be a blessing to do something, and not just for myself. The worth of my life depends on what I'm worth to others. I want to be worth something to others when I've gone on.

—Rev. Clay Evans

In every age and generation, God has provided a voice for his people. Under the divine inspiration of God, Rev. Dr. Clay Evans has been one of those voices God used to inspire, mentor, and unselfishly lead and feed so many. His influence has made an indelible impression in the hearts and minds of many of God's people.

—Rev. Maceo Woods

APRIL 2001—It was a Sunday morning around 4:30 a.m. Evans awoke ready to start the day. Four months had passed since he had retired from Fellowship. Since then, life had certainly been less hectic, especially on the Sundays. Evans didn't have to rush through a host of rituals in preparation for a busy day of pastoral ministry. On this particular Sunday in April 2001, Evans awoke with only the responsibility of being a guest preacher. The change was refreshing. Evans thrust his bedcovers off and swung his feet from the mattress to the floor. Suddenly, a sharp pain shot through his stomach. Experiencing new pains was becoming more commonplace for Evans. Time was indeed weakening Evans's seventy-five-year-old body. Perhaps, he thought, the pain would subside as he began moving around. Probably it was just stiff muscles and joints that needed warming up. He summoned the strength to force himself out of bed. Wincing, eyes tightly closed, teeth clenched, Evans began getting dressed. Again, another pain pummeled his stomach. It was excruciating. Evans could barely stand. He knew immediately that the pain was more serious than the inevitable aches that are the adversaries of aging adults.

Evans debated whether he should keep his appointment as a guest preacher at a church that morning. "But I was in so much pain," he said. He told family members about his pain, and it was decided he needed to see a doctor immediately. Evans reluctantly canceled his preaching engagement, and family members drove him to Northwestern Hospital. A doctor performed a series of blood tests. Shortly after, the attending physician came into the room, looking grave with concern. His news was grim. Evans had advanced pancreatic cancer. "They said, 'You got cancer.' I was shocked to hear it!" He would need immediate surgery. After hearing this news, family members arranged an appointment with the doctor who had diagnosed Evans to have a more detailed conversation. "So when we went in to talk to him and he laid it out," Evans recalled, "he said, 'Our experience here with pancreatic cancer after the surgery is a person only lasts about six months.'" The entire family listened in shock.

Family members scheduled an appointment at Northwestern for Evans's surgery. But Northwestern could not perform the surgery for two weeks. Driven by urgency, family members began researching other options. Evans's son-in-law, Harold Pye, took immediate action. "Harold . . . when I told him about it, he said, 'Let me get on my computer and try to find the best doctor in Illinois for pancreatic cancer.' That is what he did," Evans said. Harold's research yielded several physicians who specialized in pancreatic cancer treatment. "There were about ten in Illinois, but he came up with Dr. Doolas over at Rush Hospital." Dr. Alexander Doolas had been a medical student at Rush Hospital in 1959 and had done his residency at Presbyterian–St. Luke's Hospital in Chicago from 1960 to 1967. Between 1962 and 1964, during his residency, Doolas served as a captain in the Army Medical Corps. He had been stationed in Germany, serving as a medical officer for an artillery battalion. Now retired, Dr. Doolas in 2012 was working part-time with Rush Hospital as the Stephen Economou Professor of Surgery.

Agreeing that Doolas was the best choice to perform

Evans's surgery, the Evans family scheduled an appointment. After administering all the necessary tests, Doolas reached the same conclusion as the doctor at Northwestern: Evans had advanced pancreatic cancer. To the family's great relief, Doolas could perform the surgery within a week. Doolas was quick to point out the complexity of this surgery. "The surgery is very difficult," Doolas said. "It's the most intricate surgery that we do."[1] The surgery generally takes between four and eight hours, he said, depending upon the surgeon. "It's the most dangerous. For a general surgeon, it's the most demanding and high-risk surgery," said Doolas. At the time of Evans's surgery, Doolas had operated on between 200 and 250 patients with pancreatic cancer. He informed Evans that when it came to elderly patients, if the cancer was not cured within thirteen or fourteen months of the surgery, then the likelihood of a cure would be minimal.

The day of the surgery came. Shortly before Evans's anesthesia was administered, he lay in his hospital bed, surrounded by family and friends. He had given his family specific instructions if anything went wrong. "I don't want to be put on no machine. Or if the doctor said I'm going to be left a vegetable. I've got a pretty good relationship with God. And I was very honest about it and felt good about it. Didn't have no regrets at all. And I know I'm not perfect. I fall short of the calling. But just that confidence that it would have been all right with me." Doolas recalled how relaxed Evans seemed. "Before the surgery, Reverend Clay was joking around with people," said Doolas. "He had all the ladies around him. They loved him."

Among the close friends gathered at Evans's bedside was his close friend Rev. Jesse Jackson. Concerned about his mentor, Jackson had special instructions for Doolas, who recalled, "He takes me aside, he puts his arm around me and says, 'Doc, ain't nothing going to go wrong, is there?'" Evans also recalled the moment: "I thought he was going to scare the doctor!" Evans explained further. "That was . . . years ago, when Jesse was in his heyday and people were a little afraid of what he would say or do." Doolas took no offense and understood the concerns of Evans's family and friends.

Suddenly, hospital officials appeared at the door. It was time. Family members clutched Evans's hands. Others kissed him. Everyone stood near as the anesthesia was administered. Evans lay smiling. The voices of those who loved him best hummed sweetly as he drifted effortlessly to sleep. The surgery lasted between five and six hours. And it was successful. Doolas was confident he had removed all the cancerous tissue. The family was overjoyed to hear the news. Pleased with that report, Jackson sang Doolas's praises to the hospital's staff. "He made my standing with all the black staff in the hospital," Doolas joked. "I was a king!"

Evans spent the next few days in the hospital, recovering. Steady waves of visitors flowed in and out of his room. Family members took turns attending to Evans's needs. Old friends dropped by to offer blessings. Former church members came by to offer kind words and prayers for the pastor who had prayed for them in similar circumstances for so many years.

Even some of Evans's most persistent opponents were moved to express their wishes for his swift and full recovery. One morning, shortly after his surgery, Evans opened his eyes, and to his astonishment, there was Alderman Eddie Vrdolyak standing at his bedside. "I was amazed, because we had confrontations," Evans said. It was no secret that Rev. Clay Evans and Vrdolyak had a history of confrontations. The most bitter had occurred twenty years earlier. Jane Byrne had been elected to serve as Chicago's first female mayor between 1979 and 1983. During her candidacy, Byrne had positioned herself as a reform candidate among Chicago Democrats. Many African Americans felt Byrne's tenure as mayor was not consonant with her platform as a reform candidate and that she had carried out the same machine politics as her predecessors.[2] Evans didn't hide his negative feelings about Byrne's leadership. "I know I was not an advocate," Evans said. He often communicated these feelings from Fellowship's pulpit on Sunday mornings. Once he even criticized Byrne during a service that aired on his evening radio broadcast. He can't remember the substance of that criticism. However, his words reached the ears of some of Chicago's political elite, including Vrdolyak. Evans said he felt compelled to speak out if he discerned an injustice in Byrne's leadership. "But [Vrdolyak] did not like it, so he became very belligerent about it."

Not long after Evans's comments about Byrne were broadcast over the radio, he found himself in Vrdolyak's office. "He dared me to say anything about Jane Byrne." In response, Evans shot to his feet and pointed his index finger in Vrdolyak's face. "I stood up and said, 'You don't tell me what to say! I'm a preacher!'" Then Vrdolyak told Evans his job was to protect elected leaders like the mayor. "Well, I'm here to protect the people," Evans responded, referring to the thousands of African Americans in the city struggling for fair wages, affordable and decent housing, and equal access to education. One of Evans's preacher colleagues was also at that meeting and tried to calm Evans down. But Evans's anger burned hot. He wouldn't back down. A preacher, Evans told Vrdolyak, is obligated to speak out against injustice. Looking back on that bitter encounter, Evans observed, "You can't script me and confine me. I resented that!" Still, he found amusement in the boldness he often embodied in the face of Chicago's toughest political leaders. "I had to be reckoned with! Man, in my day!" he said, boastfully shaking both shoulders.

Given the tumultuous history between the two leaders, Evans was surprised to see Vrdolyak standing beside his hospital bed. Vrdolyak had just finished visiting an acquaintance in the hospital. He had heard that Evans was there, recovering from surgery. While the two men were not close, Evans appreciated that visit. For Evans, it was a sign that the respect the two men had for one another transcended their differences. "It's respect. You don't have to love them. You don't have to be that close. But there are certain things you do." Evans believed their confrontations afforded both of them the opportunity to be sharpened into better leaders and, more importantly, better men. "You ought to be able to communicate up and above certain things. You need it to survive. I needed Vrdolyak. And Vrdolyak needed me," Evans resolved.

After several weeks in the hospital, Evans was cleared to go home. He would need constant attention to prevent infection. "When I came home from the hospital, I had about five or six tubes in me, and they had to be taken out and cleaned every day." His family assumed responsibility for his care. Once, when reflecting on his daughter Gail's role in his recovery, Evans was brought to tears. "Gail said, 'Tell me what to do, and I'll do it,'" he recalled. His eyes welled up. His mouth quivered. His voice shook. Tears fell. Then Evans continued, "Every day, she would come kneel down by my bed, take those tubes out, clean them out, and put them back in. . . . She's a very, very good daughter. And she's good to the whole family," Evans said proudly. Dr. Doolas agreed: "Throughout the whole thing, his daughter was just outstanding."

Along with Gail, each of Evans's children made sacrifices and performed acts of love after his surgery. Evans's daughter Faith, his youngest child, took on the primary role in her father's recovery. At the time of Evans's surgery, his wife, Lutha Mae, was suffering with diabetes, and she also was bound to a wheelchair after having suffered an earlier spinal injury that prevented her from walking. With two parents unable to care for themselves, Faith decided to give up her home and move into her parents' house to become their primary caregiver. Even with two children of her own, Freeman (Bing) and Dianne, Faith decided that moving in with her parents to oversee their care was best for the entire family. Since she also had a full-time job, Faith hired a caregiver, who was responsible for helping to care for Lutha Mae. Faith also hired people to cook and clean. Some of the hired help included Bessie Tisley, Rose Denham, Patricia Bailey, Gloria Campbell, Nancy Burns, and Fanisha Sullivan. In addition to making sure her own children attended school and did their homework, Faith oversaw the housecleaning, meal preparations, doctor appointments, physical therapy, local travel and transportation when needed, and other household functions.

Faith's other siblings, Gail, Ralph, and Michael, also helped with these responsibilities when they were able. For instance, Evans's oldest son, Michael, assumed a special role when Evans regained enough strength and resumed a heavy preaching schedule. Michael became Evans's driver. Eventually, Evans's preaching schedule became so demanding that Michael also acted as his armor bearer, someone who assisted with any needs Evans had while engaging in ministry in Chicago each week. And whenever Evans traveled out of town for preaching or ministry after his surgery, his children accompanied him to provide administrative support.

Evans's son Ralph had become a talented musician. He was one of the staff musicians who had helped manage Fellowship's music ministry when Evans was still pastor. Evans especially loved to hear Ralph play the song "It's No Secret What God Can Do," the theme song for Fellowship's

Sunday-night radio broadcast. When Evans retired as pastor of Fellowship, Ralph became his personal musician, traveling with him on his numerous preaching engagements. This relationship continues today and is one example of the many acts of God's radical love and hospitality manifest through Evans's children. Truly, Rev. Clay Evans has a testimony!

During the weeks following his surgery, Evans slowly regained his strength. Throughout 2001, he had to attend a series of doctor appointments. He met with Dr. Doolas three or four times within the first few months of his surgery. Evans then went to the doctor after sixth months, and then twelve months after his surgery. He received good news at each of these appointments. Doolas did not detect any cancer, and soon Evans felt strong enough to resume an active preaching schedule.

Shortly after his surgery Evans had told Doolas that when he was strong enough, he would invite the doctor to hear him at Fellowship. That day came within the first year of Evans's surgery. Evans's successor, Rev. Charles Jenkins, extended an invitation for Evans to speak at the church he had founded. A limousine pulled up in front of Doolas's house, whisking him off to Fellowship. Not long after arriving at the church, Doolas was invited to sit in the pulpit with several of Evans's family members, including Evans's son-in-law, Harold, who first brought Doolas to the family's attention when they were searching for a surgeon. At one point during the worship service, Harold leaned over to Doolas and jokingly pointed out the significance of

Doolas's presence in the pulpit. Harold said to Doolas, "Doc, I've been married to his daughter, but I've never been up here!"

The climactic moment of the worship service came when Evans was invited to address the congregation. He retold the story of his diagnosis, testifying about all the events leading up to meeting Doolas. Then Evans invited Doolas to share a few words. Doolas had not prepared anything to say but enthusiastically acquiesced. Doolas told the congregation that Evans had been an outstanding patient. He even shared the story about Jesse Jackson pulling him aside before Evans's surgery and telling him to make sure there were no complications. Doolas later recalled being impressed with the size of the congregation and the choir. He found the entire worship service moving. "It's pretty awesome. Very awe inspiring. And the congregation was mixed," Doolas remembered. "It was whites, blacks; everybody was there."

Looking back on the whole experience, Evans is thankful he retired from Fellowship when he did. When he retired, there were no indications he was ill. "It was good timing, because I had just turned the church over to Jenkins. I wouldn't have been able to carry on anyway. But with God's timing, I had just put Jenkins in place, and I could go on without worrying how my baby, 'The Ship,' was doing." Interestingly, Evans's battle with pancreatic cancer did not make him think any more or less about death. As Evans retorted, "That's why I got saved—not only for here, but beyond here, immortality."

Several years following his surgery, Evans was eating well, preaching regularly, and not in pain. Doolas was elated about Evans's progress. "After a couple of years, no complaints, no nothing, I was very encouraged. After about five years, I was like, 'He's cured!'" Doolas exclaimed. According to Doolas, the five-year mark after pancreatic-cancer surgery is generally held to be the indicator that someone will survive. "Once you live five years, you're essentially cured," he said. "That's what we consider cured in pancreatic cancer." Doolas believed Evans's faith played a significant role in his recovery. "I think faith is very important. Good vibrations. I think it helps the immune system. But it's not the only thing. It takes a combination of everything." Doolas is particularly impressed with the active preaching ministry Evans has maintained after his surgery. Until recently Evans preached in Chicago or in other parts of the state almost every Sunday. At times, he even traveled to other parts of the country to preach. "He keeps on going," Doolas bragged. "He's enjoying himself and traveling and speaking. It's great."

In June 2017, Evans turned ninety-two, and when his health allows he still preaches on Sundays as often as he can. Many might caution Evans to slow down in his older age. But as far as Evans is concerned, he retired from pastoring but not preaching. Preaching, he said, is his calling as long as he still has breath. "God let me get up out of that bed at Rush to be a blessing to do something, and not just for myself. The worth of my life depends on what I'm worth to others. I want to be worth something to others when I've gone on."

Evans has mentored hundreds of men and women who have gone on to serve in ministerial and other leadership capacities in Chicago and across the country. These men and women, whose lives and careers bear the indelible imprint of Evans's mentorship, are carrying the mantle he bequeathed to them, embodying the same entrepreneurial and generous spirit that characterized Evans's half-century pastorate. Evans boasted of his sons and daughters in ministry and former church members, saying, "Once a Ship-ite, always a Ship-ite. Wherever you go, you might leave this church and go somewhere else, so much of me will be in you, my teaching and whatnot, that you'll never forget it."

NOTES

1. Dr. Alexander Doolas, phone interview by the author, 2012, Chicago.

2. Frederick C. Harris, *The Price of the Ticket: Barack Obama and the Rise and Decline of Black Politics* (Oxford: Oxford University Press, 2012), 45.

18

LAST OF THE BLUES PREACHERS?

There were people who heard me sing, and they identified me as a singer, and it was hard for them to iden-
tify me as a preacher. . . . I'm not a singer. I'm a preacher
who happens to sing, pray, and counsel.

—Rev. Clay Evans

Reverend Evans created a "whosoever church"
founded upon relationality. This church was a house of
blues where anybody and everybody could enter in and
find healing and refuge.

—Johari Jabir

SUNDAY, AUGUST 26, 2012—Rev. Clay Evans sat calmly
in the pulpit at Six Grace Presbyterian Church on 600 East
35th Street in Chicago. The small sanctuary was full of people gathered to hear the city's most legendary living pastor
preach. I happened to be serving as the temporary pulpit

supply pastor for this marvelous congregation while they searched for a new pastor. I beamed with pride as I officiated the service with Reverend Evans sitting beside me. It was the first and only time Reverend Evans and I were in a pulpit together for a Sunday church service.

Church members and visitors waited with excitement throughout the service, anticipating the moment when Evans would stand to preach. Then, finally, the moment arrived. Evans rose slowly from his chair. He motioned to his son Ralph at the piano to begin playing. Evans stood very still, hardly moving. He looked fragile. He was no longer able to dance across the pulpit. It was clear to many that the earthly shell of the man standing in the pulpit that Sunday was fading, succumbing to the inevitabilities of time. But suddenly, Evans let out a smooth, soft groan in tune and tempo with the pianist. The congregation clapped loudly. Some rose to their feet, others smiled, and still others shouted. It was classic Clay Evans, singing just as powerfully as he always had. Time, it seemed, had no dominion over Evans's gifts. He stood like a strong tower, a little older but strong.

Since Evans retired from Fellowship in 2000, he has maintained a regular preaching schedule. He has preached an average of three Sundays a month during the last fifteen years. "I've been preaching here and there, just about every Sunday, somewhere," said Evans. That the ninety-two-year-old cancer survivor has maintained such a rigorous preaching schedule during his retirement years is indeed a feat. Many of the pastors he has mentored personally or through his national ministry have been quick to extend preaching invitations to Evans in his retirement. "So now, since I'm not pastoring, all across the country they're opening doors for me," Evans said about his sons and daughters in the ministry. Often, Evans accepts preaching invitations to support young pastors who are just starting out in ministry. "Some of these little fellows just got started. I want to encourage them because someone encouraged me. We are debtors. . . . We talk about being debt free. But you will always owe somebody. Your mother gave birth to you. Somebody did something for you to help you be where you are today. And we ought to feel obligated to others," Evans admonished.

Though Evans has ministered all over the country and the world, he is humbled to receive invitations to even the smallest congregations, saying, "I don't worry about the size of the church. Sometimes it's one hundred or two hundred. I've preached to thousands." Evans is clear about his purpose in this season of his life and ministry: "My calling is not to do the hard preaching I used to do. I can do a little. But my purpose is counseling, to be an inspiration to younger fellows."

Rev. Larry Roberts Sr. remembers when he first learned how rigorous of a preaching schedule Evans kept in his retirement: "In 2003, when I became pastor of Trinity All Nations, he was just retiring from pastoring and was in such demand to speak across the country. I called his office and requested him to speak for Palm Sunday. His secretary said he had about fifteen requests."[1] Evans knows that at his age, each time he steps into the pulpit could be his last. But he is determined to preach until he is no longer physically able. Evans quotes the apostle Paul's words to the Corinthian church: "Paul says, in so many words, 'I must preach or perish'" (1 Corinthians 9:16). Evans explained, "So you can die other than physical death. You know the worst kind of dying? It's your soul. The soul is the most important part of a person. . . . When your soul is dead, you have no passion, no mercy. You are dead walking around."

Evans's close friend Minister Louis Farrakhan offered a similar explanation of Evans's preaching in his twilight years. For Farrakhan, as for Evans, those who have been called to preach are called to preach as long as they have breath:

See, it says that he's driven of a power bigger than himself. How do you retire from preaching God's word? How do you retire when the scripture says my people are destroyed for the lack of knowledge? What should he do? Sit up in the house and wait for the angel of death to call him in? Not my brother. He says, "I'm going to work until I can't work no more. I'm gonna give guidance until my tongue is ceased. And if my tongue ceases, I'll write it. . . . But as long as I'm alive, I'll be found doing the work of God."

That's my brother. . . . His will is "I'm not gonna go out like a little wimp. As strong as I was in my youth, I'll be stronger than that on the day that my Lord calls me home." So if he can get up and move about, his legs may be a little weaker. . . . "What did you say? Oh, say it again a little louder. My hearing may have gone. My eyes may be dimmed. But my love for Jesus Christ is stronger now than it ever was." And that's the force that makes my brother keep on moving until the Lord says, "Come in."[2]

I am blessed to say I witnessed in person Rev. Clay Evans standing in a pulpit and illuminating the scriptures, tugging at the hearts of his listeners, and drawing them into closer communion with Jesus Christ. For those who are fortunate enough to hear Evans preach these days, they are witnesses to more than an old man preaching passionately. As a ninety-two-year-old minister who was born in the segregated South to sharecropping parents, Evans is literally one of the last of his kind.

As one of the countless African Americans who were a part of the Great Migration and as one of those whose southern religious culture helped transform the religious landscapes of northern cities like Chicago, Rev. Clay Evans is definitely one of the last of his kind—one of the last living blues preachers from his era. However, Minister Louis Farrakhan is rightly suspicious of any claims that Evans is the last of his kind. In terms of the social, cultural, and political realities that shaped blues preachers of the middle of the twentieth century, Evans may indeed be among the last. However, Farrakhan insisted that Rev. Clay Evans represents an important paradigm of ministry that must be learned from and built upon for the sake of black lives and all lives today. Farrakhan poignantly surmised:

> If he's the last of the breed, the world is going to hell. Because the pain is worse now than it was then. The grief is worse now than it was then—the loss of jobs, the loss of friendship, the loss of your children to gangs and drugs and violence. How could he be the last of that kind of preacher? Oh no. No, no, no. His ministry is the foundation of a new breed of preacher that understands the pain of the people and preaches to give comfort to those who mourn. Huh? No. He's not going out of style. No. He is the style! He sets the style![3]

Farrakhan's feelings about the challenges African Americans, especially, face in the twenty-first century are not unfounded. Videos of police brutality and fatal shootings of blacks in and beyond Chicago have gained national attention in recent years. This racial terror has gripped US culture and inspired movements such as Black Lives Matter. Many communities are now mourning police brutality, shootings, and other forms of racial terror against African Americans. Therefore, Farrakhan is right. Blues preaching and blues preachers like Rev. Clay Evans are needed desperately today. Regardless of whether Evans is the last living blues preacher from his era, his legacy will certainly minister to the world long after his mortal journey. As black lives continue to face the horrors of racial violence in the United

States, Evans's witness will leave behind instructions for liberating ways forward.

In the sunset years of his ministry and life, Rev. Clay Evans is motivated by an abiding conviction that one can find in every season, in every moment, in every breath an opportunity to be used in service to God. He knows now that it's no secret what God can do. And that fundamental conviction about what God can do is what keeps Evans motivated, energized, and inspired to continue preaching and serving God as he approaches the ripe age of one hundred years. Incredibly, at his age, Evans believes that there is still much work for him to do. "You never just get somewhere and stay. Now . . . I'm deteriorating, decaying from the physical. But I hope to be stronger in the spiritual. The outward appearance, this body is decaying, deteriorating. But if the Lord gives me spiritual strength . . . I want to grow in wisdom and in knowledge," Evans testified.

His preaching these days reflects the accumulated growth in wisdom and knowledge gathered over the course of a lifetime. The elder now admonishes the young to seek a balance between the head and the heart in preaching, and a balance between theory and practice in living out the gospel. Sagaciously, Evans counseled:

> I've come to the conclusion that your intellect and your emotion ought to balance. Don't be so intellectual and so cold that you have no emotion. Don't be so emotional that you have no intellect. Somehow or another, they have to balance. That's how we were as a church.

275

And we started off that way. Have a good time on the inside. We shouted and jumped and danced on Sunday. But during the week, put some leather on your gospel—visit the sick, feed the hungry, all those kinds of things that are positive. Get involved!

Surely, then, it seems that Rev. Clay Evans *is* and *is not* the last of his kind. He is among the last surviving members of his generation of southern black migrant blues preachers. But he is also an inspiration for the kinds of leaders needed in this generation—leaders whose labors are principled enough, selfless enough, loving enough, and courageous enough to leave impressions deep enough to live beyond those leaders' mortal journeys.

When people now and in the generations to come remember Rev. Clay Evans's words, when they recount his ministry, when they listen to his recorded voice, when they recall the miraculous things God did through this once mute now muse of a man, those same people, when they reflect on how God guided Clay Evans through his and their own terrors, fears, insecurities, adventures, strange lands, loves, hopes, humiliations, failures, and victories—they will come to know what Clay Evans has come to know: that it's no secret what God can do!

As people come to know this truth more fully each day, and as they testify to others about it, they become for this generation what Rev. Clay Evans was for the last generation: blues preachers who strive in each moment to use what God has given them to get involved, to help others, to leave the world better than how they found it. They will become living legends whose inspiring legacies are the inheritance of future generations. And one day, these messengers of hope will experience with Rev. Clay Evans the reward of seeing the fruits of their labors grow and be harvested in their own lifetimes: cities transformed, ministries launched, careers begun, lives changed, bridges mended, lost hopes recovered, shattered dreams repaired, past horrors conquered, old pains healed, self-love finally embraced. These modern blues preachers, symbols of God's love in each generation, will one day survey their fruit, their life's harvest, and will rest content and humbled in the sweet, blessed knowledge that their works shall not die with them.

Notes

1. Rev. Larry Roberts Sr., written response solicited by author, 2012.
2. Minister Louis Farrakhan, interview by the author, 2012, Rev. Clay Evans's home, Chicago.
3. Minister Louis Farrakhan, interview.